FORUM FAVORITES

Volume 2

1988

Al-Anon Family Group Headquarters, Inc./New York

Forum Favorites
© Al-Anon Family Group Headquarters, Inc. 1982

Post Office Box 862
Midtown Station
New York, N.Y. 10018-0862

Seventh Printing

Library of Congress Catalog Card No. 82-73095
ISBN-910034-52-4

Approved by
World Service Conference
Al-Anon Family Groups

Printed in the United States of America

Contents

July—Living by Glimpses
Live the program fully   *137*

September—The Up-Hill Road
Acceptance comes from realism   *138*

October—Do You Pass the Buck?
Repay your obligations   *139*

November—Winnie the Pooh and Al-Anon
Al-Anon will get you   *140*

December—Christmas Can Be Every Day
Study of literature brings happiness   *141*

1967
January—Value of a Wastebasket
Toss away misconceptions   *143*

February—Enter to Learn—Go Forth to Teach
Live on a two-way street   *144*

March—Tale of Two Frogs
Do the best you can   *146*

April—Thoughts on Waste
Don't just skim Al-Anon literature   *147*

May—Adding a Cubit to Our Stature
Free yourself from resentments   *148*

June—Which Is in Control— You or Panic?
Facing fears brings solution   *149*

July—Peace Within Ourselves
Get the right perspective   *151*

August—Twelfth Step Warm-up
Don't expect instant success   *152*

September—Bounty of Al-Anon
Program sheds light in unexpected places   *153*

October—Mark Twain's Cat
Follow program persistently   *155*

November—The Best Years of Our lives
Time brings freedom and perspective   *156*

December—Christmas and Al-Anon
Help, given and taken, makes Al-Anon work   *157*

January—Where Does Twelfth Step Work End?
It is endless and endlessly satisfying   *158*

February—Getting Fit to Live
Program works the miracle   *160*

March—Putting Away Childish Things
One never graduates from Al-Anon   *161*

April—Thoughts on Stretching the Mind
Al-Anon showed me a better life   *163*

May—Look for a Long Time
Detached study shows real values   *165*

June—A Tranquilizer Highly Recommended
I saw where I was slipping   *167*

July—Don't Let It Throw You
Giving up usually leads to trouble   *169*

August—Through Other Eyes
Our only way to grow is to understand others   *171*

September—"When You Can't Do As You Would..."
Contentment is possible   *173*

October—What Do You Want?
Fear keeps us from knowing   *174*

November—One Day's FORUM Mail
It spreads a friendly world before us   *176*

December—Merry Christmas to Al-Anons and Alateens
You may never know what help you've given   *178*

1969
January—Even the Desert Blooms
Occasional discouragement isn't all bad   *180*

February—Who Would Want To Be Infallible?
There's no shame in acknowledging being wrong   *181*

March—Always Tend to Your Own Knitting
Desperation disappeared with acceptance   *183*

April—Serenity: Our Greatest
   Safeguard
Emotional upsets let evil enter   185

May—No Problem Is Without a
   Solution
You just have to look for it   187

June—Use Al-Anon's Armor to Combat
   Useless Fear
Al-Anon's program brings freedom   190

July—Al-Anon's Program Enlightens
   the World
Twelfth Step work is endless   191

August—Al-Anon Is Not a Sometime
   Thing
Why long-timers stay in Al-Anon   193

September—Al-Anons Are Modern
   Alchemists
Wasted years are turned to gold   196

October—Speak to Newcomers in Their
   Own Language
*Identification with others is our
   goal*   198

November—Al-Anon's Program Comes
   to the Rescue
Al-Anon puts a stop to self-pity   200

December—We in Al-Anon Have
   Priceless Gifts to Give
Al-Anon help is a gift above rubies   202

1970
January—Putting the Past to Work
   for Others
We can let it wreck or enrich us   205

February—Anger Can Be Friend
   Or Foe
*Sometimes anger is on the side of
   angels*   207

1963
April—Serenity Prayer, Part I   208

May—Serenity Prayer, Part II   210

June—Serenity Prayer, Part III   211

September—But for the Grace of God
*Alcoholism is an accidental illness
   which might have struck us*   213

November—Al-Anon's Three
   Important Days
*Al-Anon program removes regret,
   gives guidance and hope*   214

December—The Lord's Prayer
Contains many of the Twelve Steps   215

1967
January—Listen and Learn
Learn to cope by careful attention   216

February—Easy Does It
Makes Al-Anon work smoothly   217

March—Let Go and Let God
*—Goes hand in hand with acceptance
   of powerlessness*   218

April—Think
Only way to find proper solutions   219

June—First Things First
*Determining priorities restores order
   to daily life*   221

July—Words to Live By
Success comes from never giving up   222

August—Keep an Open Mind
Best way to get best help   223

September—Live and Let Live
We need to do both   224

October—Who Said "This Is a Selfish
   Program"?
*Program is personal rather than
   selfish*   226

November—Discussion of "We Have
   No Dues or Fees"
Where support is needed and why   227

1968
Discussion of the Twelve Steps
*(Fifth Step—May 1966, Ninth Step
   —Sept. 1960)*   228

1969
Discussion of the Twelve Traditions   247

Index of Subjects   269

Living by Glimpses

IF YOU REALLY apply the Twelve Steps of Al-Anon, every
minute of every day offers an opportunity to put them into
practice.

Acoustics are bad in my church. I have to strain to hear
the sermon. Most times I get only a phrase here and there,
so perhaps it's easy to understand why my thoughts wan-
der. Just the other day a phrase got through to me, out of
the jumble. My instant thought was, "That's pure Al-
Anon."

What I heard was, "Doing good . . . silence ignorance.
Live as freemen." In Al-Anon, "carry the message" and
"restore us to sanity." The rest of the sermon time I spent
correlating these words with the Twelve Steps and perhaps
sermonized myself. At any rate, I somehow caught a
glimpse at what living our program fully could mean.

Many times such glimpses come: as yesterday, when a
car, entering a garage well in front of me, blocked the
sidewalk. I was annoyed because I did not want to go into
the street, into traffic, to get around it. I was saying pithy
things to myself as I approached the stopped car. Just as
my blood boiled and as I got within ten feet of it, the car
smoothly rolled out of my way, leaving the walk clear.
That time, the "24 hour program" jumped to mind but I
sheepishly said to myself, "For you, it should be 24 minutes or 24 seconds."

Living by glimpses, such as these, is really what we do in
the Twelfth Step when we "practice the program in all our
daily affairs." When we do that we really are making the
program work for us and us for it.

The Up-Hill Road

THE BEST PART of Al-Anon, as I see it, is that it teaches us
to be realistic, to accept the fact that there are things we
cannot change, things we can, and encourages us to distinguish which is which.

No one says it is fun to live with alcoholism, especially
when the problem is acute. It is not fun for the alcoholic,
either, as far as that goes. But Al-Anon and AA are the two
greatest guides on coping with the situation that have yet
been devised.

Each of us has his own limit of tolerance. When that
point is reached, the fortunate one among us, through Al-
Anon's teachings, finds the courage to face his life as it is,
to stop milling around in a welter of fears, frustrations and
nightmares. When things have got as bad as they can get,
there's no way to go but up.

Al-Anon does not say it will cure the problems besetting
us. But it will, and does, help us to live more equably with
them. It does not say, "Do this, and your problems are
over." Nor does it say that even if you do all it teaches,
you'll never have another problem. In a wide reading
experience I've never found a seventy year, or even a six
month guarantee for a completely happy, problem-free
life.

What Al-Anon does is to stiffen our minds and our wills
to accept what comes, to get good out of everything by
seeing that each experience makes for spiritual growth.
Christina Rossetti expressed this acceptance in fewer words
than I: "Does the road wind up-hill all the way? Yes, to the
very end. Will the day's journey take the whole long day?
From morn to night, my friend." This is truly realism and
true acceptance of that realism.

Our up-hill road is frequently a very difficult one. But it does lead to a beautiful view if we remain faithful to Al-Anon's guideposts.

Do You Pass the Buck?

DURING WW II we spent nearly two years at an air base in Nebraska before Jack, my husband, went to the Orient. One of our great friends was the Quartermaster Captain. Jack always said he was the best QM. he'd ever met; most of them, in his long military experience, doled out supplies grudgingly, as if they were personal property. Captain Roberts issued them cheerfully.

The thing which first impressed *me* with him was the sign he had over his office: "The Buck Stops Here." In the service it's nice to know it does stop, and where.

Many times at meetings I remember Captain Roberts and his sign. I attend a daytime discussion group where many newcomers come for a time and then leave to join groups nearer their homes. Usually they are women living with an active problem; it's their first contact with Al-Anon and they are decidedly in need of help.

The first thing which impressed me when I was new to the group, and it still impresses me, is the fact that every member speaks up when she is able to help the newcomer. This was not always true of other groups of which I was a member. Usually there were two or three who seldom said anything beyond joining in saying the Lord's Prayer.

They were too inhibited, too self-distrustful, much too wrapped up in their own affairs; they said they were not "good" at Twelfth Stepping. How did they know? They never tried, as far as I could discern!

I'm sure that sometimes some experience of theirs must have matched that of the newcomer who was asking for help. But they remained silent and passed the buck to the others. Valuable help was lost many times, I'm sure.

Our responsibility in Al-Anon is to help others as we were helped. We have no professional Twelfth Steppers in Al-Anon—we wouldn't want them. But we do want the shared experience of all of us. Perhaps if there were a sign on each chair which said, "The Buck Stops Here," every member, no matter how shy, would share his experience.

Winnie-the-Pooh and Al-Anon

MANY OF US find ourselves in much the same fix as Milne's Pooh, who had promised to write a poem about Piglet's heroism and found the going difficult: "But it isn't easy," said Pooh to himself, "because Poetry and Hums aren't things which you get, they're things which get *you*. And all you can do is to go where they can find you."

So Pooh waited hopefully to see what happened, and a seven-verse poem happened, which he supposed had never been heard of before—not at least in the House at Pooh Corner.

In my very early days of Al-Anon, the First Step was very much on my mind. I thought of it constantly but found myself doing all the futile things I'd always done; I was as far from actually practicing that Step as if I'd never heard of it. Fortunately, I kept going to meetings—the place where it could find me—and eventually *it* did find *me* and I began living an Al-Anon life.

So it was with a dear friend. Dot had attended AA meetings with her husband for a long time. She was happy and satisfied with AA, saw no reason to look within herself for anything wrong in her life. Then a friend began working on her to go to Al-Anon until, finally, in protest, she thought she'd go to a few meetings to prove the friend wrong and then she'd drop it happily.

She went to Al-Anon a time or two, tongue in check, and was satisfied Al-Anon wasn't for her. But after a few meetings, it was time to change officers and she was asked to be secretary. She didn't like to refuse so she kept attending meetings and before long, Al-Anon had got a firm hold on her.

Another friend had attended Al-Anon a couple of years, and ended up chairman of the group for six months. As she went home the night new officers were chosen, she thought to herself: "I've now attended Al-Anon three years. I've learned all it teaches and I think I've graduated. I'll go next week to turn over the chairmanship and then I'll be free Wednesday nights."

But something happened that next Wednesday at her job and her first thought was, "This is where Al-Anon can keep me straight—I need it more than ever." That was a dozen years ago and she is still attending an Al-Anon group!

So with Pooh, I say, Al-Anon is a thing which *gets you*. All you need do is go where it can find you and, sooner or later, it will be your rod and your staff.

Christmas Can Be Every Day

CHRISTMAS is a time of giving, sometimes gifts, sometimes hospitality, sometimes just a sharing of personal news on a Christmas card.

Whatever it is, there is a special feeling in the air of brotherhood, a lift of the spirit, a sense of something joyous and not of every day. For weeks before the happy day, we prepare for it with all the love and thoughtfulness in our hearts.

This universal observance of the Christmas season does not mean that all our giving is confined to Christmas—far from it. It just comes to a climax then and we try a little harder to be thoughtful and generous. And we of Al-Anon are peculiarly enabled to stretch the Christmas season through all the months of the year, if we will.

The greatest gift one can make another, I believe, is the gift of hope. And to me, hope is the essence of our Al-Anon philosophy. No matter how black is our situation, Al-Anon gives us assurance that there is help for us.

It is axiomatic that you cannot give what you have not got. You cannot help another person by parroting words which you do not understand and do not believe. But you can lift another from the depths of despair by a few words of your own sure knowledge and experience.

Attending Al-Anon meetings is essential for understanding of the program but I do not believe it is enough. We have a tremendous, additional store of knowledge and experience in our Al-Anon literature.

And there's something very peculiar about that literature: every time you reread a piece of it, you get a different slant on questions and additional help as well.

If you wish to give Al-Anon's gift of hope to those still suffering, do make a thorough review of all our literature. You will be doubly blest: your own understanding will be enlarged and deepened, and you will be better able to help others.

Your gift of hope can help make Christmas every day. God Bless!

Value of a Wastebasket

WE RECENTLY MOVED, after eight years in a fairly small apartment. It's lovely to have more room, marvelous to look out on the most spectacular view of the Hudson and the Palisades in the world—but accustomed things have an annoying way of not being where I instinctively reach for them.

Like my wastebasket: for eight years it has been beside my typewriter where I can drop paper in it without looking. The other day I sat down to work on the new FORUM. I put in a fresh sheet of paper and suddenly realized the wastebasket was not there—it was still in a glut of things unsorted and unplaced. And I froze up. I could not type a word until I had stopped, hunted it up and put it in its accustomed place. This bothered me for a time because I kept thinking, "Why can't you type without a wastebasket?"

When I had thought it out, I knew I was asking the wrong question. It should have been, "Why can't you write without a wastebasket?" And I knew I couldn't. I'm sure now it's best that I can't.

To begin with, there's nothing quite so cold as a fresh piece of white paper. Others may be inspired by such a challenge but I go sort of blank. No matter how much thought I have given my piece, how well I have planned its introduction, the first few lines on a new sheet of paper never quite express what I had planned. I drop down a bit and begin over, changing a word or two, or a phrase, until I've come as close as I believe I can to what I mean to say.

By the time I have a reasonable facsimile of what I want

to say, the wastebasket is deep in false starts, each one just a little bit closer to exactness.

For days now I've been thinking of writing and wastebaskets. I also wish everyone had a compulsive habit of a mental wastebasket when talking.

If, mentally, we could sort out the irrelevant, the obscure and the distracting things which keep us from expressing our exact meaning, conversation would be a thrilling and stimulating experience.

We'd have no difficulty in interpreting to newcomers just why they are powerless over alcohol, just how they make themselves "Let Go and Let God." There'd be no obscurity, no chance for misunderstanding.

It would be the millennium if we all talked as Churchill did. But we can try, at least. Here's for more and bigger mental wastebaskets.

"Enter to Learn; Go Forth to Teach"

SOMEONE recently queried the New York Times Book Section as to the source of the maxim, "Enter to learn; go forth to teach." I cannot identify the quotation but I can accept it as a perfect blueprint for good Al-Anon membership.

Most of us, but not all of course, enter Al-Anon to learn what magic button to press to turn an uncontrolled drinker into a model of sobriety.

We often do not even know that alcoholism is a disease. We just know our lives are a mess because of it and we want it stopped—right now, and for good. Why should we tolerate excess?

We know we are doing everything in our power to stop

the drinking, to outwit the imbiber and out maneuver him so that he can't get a drink.

Every unhappy thing in our lives is laid to drinking. None of it is our fault. Naturally! We don't drink to excess and therefore we are perfect. Or were *you* different?

That's where the beginning of wisdom occurs. First we learn there is no magic button. We learn alcoholism is a disease and the alcoholic has contracted it. We learn that all our "helpfulness" is an extra burden for the alcoholic to carry.

Occasionally we get a glimmer that our wings have molted a bit here and there and our halos have dulled over the years. Gradually we have come to recognize that we ourselves are less than perfect and can use the guides provided for us.

Thus, although we entered only to learn about the magic button, we did enter to learn. We did learn, too—not what we anticipated but what would really help us in our dilemma.

And having learned a great deal of what Al-Anon teaches—there's always something new so that we never graduate—we accept the obligation to "go forth to teach."

In our new-found gratitude for the help we have received, we wish to share our experience with those still suffering, still floundering as we floundered. By guiding others in the program, we strengthen our own practice of it.

By giving of ourselves, our beliefs, our practices, we are enriched beyond measure; our Al-Anon program becomes a stronger influence in our lives and our joy in it is increased a hundredfold.

We cannot selfishly hoard our joy and our helpfulness and still live our program. Thus I cannot think of a better maxim for us to follow than "Enter to learn; go forth to teach."

Tale of Two Frogs

MARY L.S., of San Diego, Cal., sent me a marvelously imaginative tale by which she has been living.

A farmhand carelessly left a freshly-milked pail of milk in the cowshed and went off to supper. Two frogs promptly jumped in.

One frog thrashed frantically around, exhausted himself and sank, discouraged, to the bottom. The other quietly moved his front and hind legs back and forth, easily keeping his head above the surface.

Next morning the farmhand returned to find the frog happily croaking, seated on a large blob of butter! When he dumped the now useless contents, the frog joyously went about his business. And down at the bottom was the first frog—dead.

As an old-time churner (I regularly churned during the ranch years), I heartily admire that second frog. Mary is grateful to him, too. She says that when she first heard the story it had little meaning for her. But since Al-Anon it reminds her always "neither to fight nor run away—just quietly to do the best I can with serenity, and I, too, may churn my blob of butter which will save my life and sanity."

Since Mary's letter came last November—it's taken all this time to find a place for it—I've been living with the second frog, too, deeply grateful to her for making us acquainted.

I have seldom, since Al-Anon, indulged in scenes or sought release from unpleasant circumstances by boiling over. Rather, I have created more tension within mself by mentally thrashing around until I have exhausted myself, when, fortunately, Al-Anon takes over and I again see things in perspective.

Mary's frog has happily shortened this period. I may not now have butter to show for my efforts but I do attain a better quality of serenity, more quickly.

Thoughts on Waste

WHEN MY DAUGHTER was away at college she wrote some humorous verses about her roommate which have always amused me. They ended, as I remember, "I now must add, before I stop, she *squeezes toothpaste from the top!*" These lines frequently come to mind when I hear people ask for more and more new Al-Anon literature.

Everyone knows that squeezing toothpaste from the top is wasteful and leads to difficulty as the paste is used. I used to do it, until I found I frequently was squeezing it messily through a break in the tube and it was virtually impossible to get all the paste out.

When I took the trouble to squeeze from the bottom—and I grant it is more trouble—it always came out neatly from the opening provided and I could use the entire contents of the tubes.

So, back to our Al-Anon literature; many times, when these requests for new pamphlets come, or when a group has got itself into difficulties and writes for help, a small amount of consideration shows that the situation has already been covered—the solution suggested. Either the writers have never read the literature, or they have simply skimmed it "from the top."

Spring is upon us—a good time to take a fresh look at our Al-Anon Conference Approved literature, so that the practice of our program may have new stimulus and growth, to make it match that of the burgeoning world about us.

A thoughtful review of our literature will not only repay you personally, in deepening your understanding of yourself and your family, it will enable you to be a better help to those still in need. It is too good to receive only the "once over lightly" treatment.

Adding a Cubit to Our Stature

DON'T YOU AGREE there's a tie between not practicing the First Step and holding resentments? Perhaps one leads inevitably to the other but both stand on their own feet as menaces to good practice of Al-Anon.

We are told that "No man, by taking thought, can add a cubit to his stature." Since a cubit varies from 17+ to 20+ inches, I can't see who would like to add one physically. But I do believe most of us would like to add several spiritually. And it is exactly by taking thought that we can do so.

Today let's think of resentments. To me, harboring resentments is a lot like encasing ourselves in a surrounding shell like the bullet-proof shield they show on TV where nothing, not even high-powered ammunition, penetrates. Nothing enters; nothing goes forth—everything bounces off.

Holding resentments is much like that. Nothing changes; our reaction is always the same to a given situation. And as long as we foster and feed the resentment by a customary reaction, just so long do we remain static, or grow worse.

If we resent slips—and I don't expect anyone to welcome them—and react by raising Cain ourselves, we don't progress.

If we work on the acceptance of alcoholism as a disease and train ourselves to accept a slip as a symptom of that disease, we are on the way to overcoming resentment of the slip.

We are freeing ourselves from a bit of the prison we have erected about ourselves. Some little help has a chance to penetrate our shield, even though it is only the thought that "This, too, shall pass." If we recognize that the situation will not last forever, we can better cope with it.

Thus, by giving thought, instead of reacting in an established, unhelpful way, we can increase our tolerance, reduce our resentment.

Few of us, if any, can change overnight. We are not snakes who shed outworn skins in a moment and instantly emerge in shining new ones.

We may have to set stakes to measure our forward progress. But by giving sufficient thought to what Al-Anon teaches us, we can gradually add to our spiritual stature, one infinitesimal bit at a time, until those bits add up to a cubit.

Which Is in Control—You or Panic?

"FEAR IS THE BEGINNING of all weakness." I don't remember where I picked that up but the more thought it is given, the truer it is that fear is the beginning of most, if not of all, weaknesses.

Robert Frost expressed the same thought in a slightly different way: "The people I am most scared of are the people who are scared."

If your mind is in a welter of fear, no matter of what, you cannot possibly do a job of clear thinking and arrive at a good solution. I am not speaking of the kind of fear of accident which makes us wait for green lights at street crossings instead of darting out in the middle of traffic. That is only common sense.

I do mean the kind of fear which envelops us when we forget that today is all the time we have, when we get ourselves into a quivering mess of fear of tomorrow or next year or ten years from now.

That kind of fear can do nothing but harm. All it can do is weaken us, prevent us from making our best effort to plan sanely and wisely for whatever comes. The worst thing about such a fear is that each time we allow ourselves to become a prey to it, it makes it easier to succumb a second time, and a third, until we become afraid of everything.

The solution is not easy. But there is a solution.

Should you find yourself faced with a situation which normally would throw you into a nervous collapse of uncontrolled fear, quietly sit down and try to put everything out of your mind for a bit. Then face your fear: analyze it; pursue it until you determine what really is the absolute worst that could happen.

Perhaps this will be too difficult for you to do alone. If so, by all means talk it over with someone in whom you have confidence, someone who has had a like experience and is competent to help—not just a hand-holder, a shoulder-patter, and a listening post.

Then, having pursued your fear to its bitter end, and having recognized it for the craven thing it probably is, there is no further place to go but onwards.

Courage will replace the nameless fears which are so frightening. Calmness will come to enable you to face whatever comes. You—not panic—will be in control.

Peace Within Ourselves

MARGARET MEAD once said that we are the first generation
in history which is asked to ponder the entire world's ills
with our morning coffee. Communication is so instant
today that every disaster comes upon us with the shock of
current happening.

When men went to the Crusades, or when clipper ships
sailed to the Orient, news of disasters was brought home
years later with the cushion of time behind it, and thus was
easier to bear.

In spite of this, we do not want to shut ourselves away
from the world—most of us would, indeed, find it impossible to do so. Our salvation lies in getting things into
proper perspective, so that when the world's woes hit us at
the same time we are under personal strain, we can keep
from going under by concentrating on what is possible for
us to do to ease the strain. The three parts of the Serenity
Prayer are our best help here.

"Every crime is punished," wrote Emerson; "the swin-
dler only swindles himself . . . there's no penalty for
virtue, wisdom, love, beauty. When these are considered in
their purest sense, they bring the sweetest of rewards—
peace within ourselves."

If we keep swindling ourselves by eternally struggling
against the things we cannot change, we are the worst
losers. It is a sad consequence that those about us lose also,
because we are not creating a tranquil home.

But if we can lift ourselves above these crippling distrac-
tions, these unhappy distortions, we can free our minds
and renew our spirits to improve everything around us.

If we successfully suppress impotent rebellion and concentrate only upon achieving a quiet calm, we'll have that greatest gift of all, "peace within ourselves." Everyone about us will share in our serenity.

Twelfth Step Warm-Up

HAVE YOU EVER seemed to fail on a Twelfth Step call, retired within yourself and decided you were just no good at it? If so, do remember this: good Twelfth Step work isn't always accomplished easily. Except for a fortunate few, most of us have to practice, and practice!

It has been proved, also, that seeming failure seldom is actual failure. Sometimes the person you call on isn't ready for help. Or perhaps he doesn't identify with you. (Even the best talks we hear in group meetings understandably fail to identify with every listenener.)

But the few words you say of what Al-Anon has done for you may kindle a tiny spark to light the darkness. Buried deep, perhaps even out of mind, they may remain in the subconscious until the need is imperative.

That spark then bursts into flame and the person is ready for the hope and help Al-Anon can so generously give, through you or some other Al-Anon member.

Uninformed people living with the problem of alcoholism, trying to cope with it all alone, not unnaturally are frequently touchy. Personally, even with sponsors as experienced as Lois and Dot, I was a prickly pear for months, shutting them off as frequently as I could. But they refused to entertain hurt feelings—kept the contact and waited until I was ready to open my eyes and my mind.

It is better, I believe, to offer help too soon than to risk being too late. Our shoulders broaden in Al-Anon: we can accept rebuffs and not be crippled by resentments. We don't want just to stand by like the two hesitant ladies who sat by the lakeshore, watching a drowning man come up for the third time and said, "Oh dear, oh dear, why DOESN'T he cry for help!"

Should your helpful offer be unwelcome, you easily can withdraw. Later, if the person comes to you and asks to learn more of the program, you then can speak freely.

If assistance is asked of someone else, that is fine and not an occasion for hurt feelings or a conclusion that you are not good at Twelfth Stepping. Perhaps it's because you needed a little more practice. Perhaps you pushed too hard, too soon, in your enthusiasm, and he wasn't quite ready.

If a response is negative, console yourself with the thought that you have lit a spark and didn't let someone sink before he cried for help.

Bounty of Al-Anon

ONE REWARD for the consistent observance of the Al-Anon program is the unexpected light it frequently sheds upon ideas and problems apart from the program itself.

Like the time I wrote about before when I fumed because a car down the street blocked the sidewalk and I thought I'd have to go into the road to pass it. Just as I approached it, with ten extra pounds of blood pressure from exasperation, the car drove off; my way was clear. I was disturbed when "Easy Does It" and "The 24 Hour Program" popped into my mind: I'd got all worked up over something which never happened.

A more startling coincidence occurred just the other day which cast light on an idea I'd cherished a very long time.

A thousand years ago, more or less, when I was in school, a professor told of Margaret Fuller's proclamation, "I accept the Universe!" He went on to repeat Carlyle's comment, when he heard of her announcement: "She damn well better!"

Although I knew Margaret Fuller was considered a brilliant woman, a Transcendentalist, one of the earliest champions of equal rights for women and among the foremost critics of her time, I immediately put her down as a silly show-off. Carlyle's comment seemed well merited, if abrupt. All these years I've had a smug sense of superiority whenever I've thought of her.

Last week, something brought her to mind. As usual, my first thought was, "Silly show-off. What else could she do?" I was not thinking of Al-Anon, at least not consciously. But instantly, and for the first time, it flashed upon me that she had actually gained the wisdom I pray for "to accept the things I cannot change."

My long-established smugness was shattered. Suddenly bereft of an idea which had long been part of me, I felt a deep sense of chagrin that I had so greatly misjudged another person. I was indeed grateful it couldn't matter to Margaret Fuller—dead more than a hundred years—what I had thought of her. But it did give me pause when I wondered what other misconceptions I still might cherish, ones which could matter.

The bounty of Al-Anon, to me, is the power it gives us to change thoughts and habits of a lifetime, to shed old prejudices, and to gain new insights into murky places.

Mark Twain's Cat

*We should be careful to get out of an experience only
the wisdom that is in it, and stop there, lest we be like the
cat that sits down on a hot stove-lid. She will never sit
down on a hot stove-lid again—and that is well, but also
she will never sit on a cold one anymore.*

Mark Twain

How many times have you tried something, failed dis-
mally, and said, "Never again! That's not for me." Perhaps
it isn't and perhaps it is—it may be a cold stove-lid which
just looked hot. Too often, I believe, we shut ourselves
away from accomplishment by giving up too readily.

If you are inhibited, shy and easily embarrassed, you
probably find it difficult to speak at open meetings; if you
are a perfectionist, very likely you have little patience with
yourself at being less than a golden-tongued orator.

Thus you may prefer to make your contribution to the
group and the program by helping with chores. This is all
very well; the jobs have to be done and you contribute to
the smooth running of the group by doing them.

But should you stop there? Making coffee never explained our program to anyone. Your experience in Al-
Anon, or the particular thing which most helped you,
perhaps may be just the thing which would bring the
whole program into focus for someone else.

At first, telling your story might be like sitting on a hot
lid. But as you discipline yourself to speak in public, you
most likely will find that the lid becomes cooler and
cooler.

A once-over-lightly approach to our program accom-
plishes nothing. You have to persist in practicing the

difficult parts, as well as the easy ones. Persistence, not quitting, pays off.

If you tackle those things which are most difficult for you, one at a time, instead of plunging wholesale into general reform, you'll have a greater chance of success.

You can learn to distinguish which lids stay hot and which cool off.

The Best Years of Our Lives

IT'S SADDENING to think so many people are afraid of age. Today's emphasis in the U.S. and seemingly in England with Twiggy, the Beatles, Mods and all that genre, is on youth—not "flaming youth" as between wars but just youth.

Such great importance given to lack of years makes many regret theirs have increased. Lately I heard a man of 50-odd say, seriously, that by then "the best years" are gone.

This seems nonsense to me. Worse, I feel it is idiotic. I don't believe I feel so strongly about this because I have "silver threads among the gold." I no longer do. They've changed from silver to ivory. But even when they all shone pure gold I felt the same.

Probably I owe this feeling to the most brilliant man I ever knew—a diagnostician and researcher, in his mid-forties. I was his secretary, in my mid-twenties.

One day I found him reading a magazine I considered trifling. He'd come early to read it before it was put in the reception room and carelessly carried off.

Horrified, I said, "WHAT are YOU doing with that trash? I don't read it and I haven't a tenth your brain!" He smiled and said, "My dear, I'm 45. I consider that by now I cannot harm my brain. I feel I can do with it as I like."

That thought gave me pause for days. I decided I would never be afraid of any birthday—30, 40, even 70 or 80. Each would find me ready, perhaps would free me of some restriction but surely would give me a better perspective of what was important and what nonessential. Happily, that is exactly how it is working out.

How can we put our best effort into what we do if part of our mind is concentrated on regretting lost youth, or if part is off with the gypsies speculating on a future of more years? This why our 24-hour program is so logical and so valuable.

No one of us knows how much time we'll have. But even if the present moment is bad, our program shows us how to live through it without giving up. We have gained resources to help us.

If we live each day completely, to the best of our ability, according to our program, not looking back in regret nor forward in despair, we are sure to attain maturity. And no really mature person, I believe, can agree that the best years of our lives are over until there are no more years.

Christmas and Al-Anon

EVER THINK how much Christmas and Al-Anon have in common? Both are based on love; both bring joy and hope to the world, lift our spirits and fill our hearts with kindness toward all.

Christmas climaxes a year in which we may or may not have done all we could for our fellow-man. It frequently inspires us to think of new ways we can give of ourselves. It gives us impetus toward doing more for others.

Christmas is not only a day—it is a time and it is a feeling. This time and this feeling are where it is most like Al-Anon. Our fellowship has restored us to mental and spiritual health, returned joy to our lives and made us keenly aware that we need keep practicing Al-Anon principles daily, in all our affairs.

We cannot let our program be a one-day anniversary, no matter how great and good the occasion we celebrate. We need to "get it and give it," every day in some way. We cannot hoard it to ourselves, or it will wither away. The more we give of the program to another, the more meaningful it is to us and the stronger we become in rooting out weakness in ourselves.

Thus it seems to me that Al-Anon is a year round Christmas—we get help and we give it. We are happy and we show others how to attain happiness. We are blessed and we share our blessings.

May every Christmas joy be yours and may Al-Anon strengthen and guide you all through the year.

Where Does Twelfth Step Work End?

. . . it begins with you but did you ever wonder just how far it stretches?

You know the joy and the thrill of seeing hope rekindle when, after a talk at an open meeting, people come to say you have cast light in a dark place. But does the help stop there?

The longer I am in Al-Anon and the more letters to the FORUM I read, the more I realize that helping someone never stops with the first person helped.

I am an utter moron at Physics and cannot understand

that a ripple, caused by a stone cast into water, goes on and on, into infinity.

Even were the stone cast into the sea, I'd think the ripple soon would peter out; if cast into a pond, surely it must stop at the shore? But it doesn't take Physics to make me see the widespread effect of Al-Anon Twelfth Stepping.

At my first meeting, a stranger changed my life by her talk; I've never told of that meeting without having four to a dozen people—AAs as well as Al-Anons—tell me I'd taken an intolerable burden from them. How many more have been helped by these dozens (and the dozens reached by those dozens) it's impossible to guess. Her story and its effect on me must, by now, have reached hundreds and thousands, I'm sure.

When she made that talk, I'm equally sure she had no idea of affecting anyone beyond the eight or ten members there.

One cannot know what effect something will have. I remember telling in Cleveland of the countless things I did to keep my husband from the first drink.

I had planned my talk carefully, had typed it out several times to boil it down and gone over it countless times so that I could speak easily.

But as I recounted my endless, futile attempts, quite spontaneously I added, "The only thing I didn't do was the one thing I should have done—NOTHING."

Years later, at Toronto, someone spoke of the great help she'd had from my Cleveland talk: "What you said about doing nothing has kept me from trying to run things ever since! I'll never forget it and never stop practicing it."

Someone quoted in a letter to the FORUM, years ago, "Fear knocked at the door. Faith answered and lo!, there was no one there." It was printed as a Stopper. Many times since, I've heard it quoted at meetings.

Also I know of a young woman who has lived by it for the eight years since she read it in the FORUM. Furthermore she is teaching her three children to live by it, too.

God bless the person who sent it in. She can't know how much good she did for so many but the good still carries on.

Perhaps Shakespeare said it all, more concisely, in "How far that little candle throws his beams!" But eventually the little beam can no longer be seen. Al-Anon Twelfth Step influence, however, goes on and on, gaining strength as it reaches each new person. May its impetus never lessen until there no longer is need anywhere in this whole world.

Getting Fit to Live

A BOOK which Bill, co-founder of AA, frequently refers to as an influence in his life and in the formation of AA, is William James's *The Varieties of Religious Experience*.

Because of my great love and admiration for Bill, my endless gratitude for his part in the miracle of AA, I recently read it. It more than repaid me.

James's answer to part of a questionnaire he filled out in 1904 particularly impressed me:

"Q. Do you believe in personal immortality? Ans. Never keenly but more strongly as I grow older.

"Q. If so, why? Ans. Because I am just getting fit to live."

James at that time was 62!

Whether or not one believes in personal immortality is not important here. But "Because I am just getting fit to live" should be graven, I believe, on the hearts of every Al-Anon member.

Perhaps you were different—not as I was—pre-Al-Anon. On looking back now, from considerable experience in our fellowship, I can readily see that I was not really fit to live before it. I was withdrawn, resentful, incapable of a healthy, outgoing life. My own problems and unhappiness occupied me fully. It was not a life.

Every group to which I have belonged, every Al-Anon I've really talked with, has taught me things I needed to know or to remember in order to be fit to live.

Every letter I have received in my work on the FORUM has added its share; I have been favored beyond my deserts—I gratefully acknowledge it.

But each of us does have the program to follow; if truly lived and honestly followed, it can make all of us fit to live.

If it worked for the mess I was, it can work for you.

It did work for me, thank God. But in case you think I'm measuring myself for a halo, I'm not. By working for me, I mean the old bitterness is gone; the self-preoccupation is shattered; my horizons are widened to include the world. If that is not succeeding, if it is not becoming fit to live, remember, I am still in Al-Anon, still working at the program and it will carry me farther, as long as I stay with it.

The more you put into it, by study of the literature, by going to meetings, and by extending a generous helping hand to anyone in difficulty with some part of the program, the more fit you'll make yourself to live.

Putting Away Childish Things

REMEMBER WHEN we did "number work" back in the early grades? The multiplication tables and the "gazintas"? Perhaps you carefully said "two goes into six three times" but in our young words we rattled it off so that it came out gazintas.

All that was fine for that age. But Einstein could never have figured his complicated equations on number work, though he undoubtedly began his schooling with it. It took advanced study and years of higher mathematics as a foundation for his later work.

Entering Al-Anon is like our number work! It's a beginning we all must make in order to go on to other things. At first, just learning that we are not alone in our problem is enough.

Then we are told alcoholism is a disease for which we are not responsible. With this, the burden of failure begins to be lifted from us and resentment of the alcoholic begins to drop away. Who, in his right mind, can hold anyone responsible for a disease he had contracted?

With these three basics (knowledge we are no longer alone, have not failed in our jobs as mates, and alcoholism is a disease) we glimpse, and are anxious to return to, a normal life. They are Al-Anon's first gift.

Perhaps just these three facts are enough to enable some people to keep on an even keel for years and for their lives to be like the old fairy tales, happy ever after. Perhaps— just perhaps.

To my mind, old habits of thought, old patterns of behavior, are so strongly ingrained that I believe these three facts constitute only a firm foundation for a new approach to life.

It takes valiant, continuous work to overcome entrenched ideas, especially where we have always thought ourselves right and others wrong.

Resentments and self-pity are not always killed with a single blow—not even usually. We frequently believe they are. But we learn to our horror they more likely are akin to the Hydra who, when one head was cut off, grew two in its place.

Sometimes people tire of Al-Anon. They think they have learned all it can teach. They believe they have "graduated" from it and prefer to do something else each week, rather than go to a meeting. So they stop going.

Without the stimulation of the group, and without the impetus toward Al-Anon thinking provided at meetings, most of them soon find themselves slipping into old ways of thought. The fortunate ones return before much damage is done.

There is so much depth to the Al-Anon program, so many ways to interpret its teachings, that it is difficult for me to see how any one person could ever think he knew it all.

The odds I sometimes see on the chances of holding certain combinations of cards in bridge hands always make me dizzy. So it is when I think of the number of different applications people have made of the same Al-Anon principle. They are endless—and endlessly helpful.

I am happy I learned the three basic facts in Al-Anon. But, just as Einstein needed more than "number work" for his equations, so do I need more and deeper study for my adult life in Al-Anon. I hope I have "put away childish things" and never stop learning, by continued advanced study, the infinite riches of the Al-Anon philosophy.

Thoughts on Stretching the Mind

OLIVER WENDELL HOLMES's memory had a special place in my youth. My father was a member of the last class he taught at Harvard Medical School. As a memento, he copied out a whole stanza from "The Boys" on the flyleaf of his Collected Poems, autographed it and gave it to my father.

Perhaps that fact, plus my long ago, superficial reading of him, contributed to my great surprise when I came upon a quotation from him recently: "Stretch the mind and it never goes back." That didn't fit anything I ever associated with Holmes but it did bring me up short.

"Stretch the mind." What other aim should life have? I don't want to seem pedantic nor be overly "Stern-Daughter-of-the-voice-of God"-ish, but I do believe all our experiences should contribute to a wider, deeper understanding of life and a better ability to adjust ourselves to it.

That is why our program is so precious and helpful to me. Before Al-Anon, I was in constant rebellion against the turmoil in my life because of my inability to accept and adjust to difficulties connected with alcoholism.

I was over-fond of dismissing the whole thing as, "This is too dusty a life—I was meant for better things."

Strangely enough, I was exactly right; I WAS meant to have a better life. Every one of us is. But that better life has to be earned.

It took Al-Anon to show me how to live this better life. Instead of constantly rolling around the idea of what was due me, Al-Anon opened my eyes to the surprising fact that *I had made my life what it was.* My own rebellion, my resentments, had blinded and sickened me.

Al-Anon—and it didn't come easily nor quickly—showed me that my life could be what I made it. By truly accepting my powerlessness over alcohol, by realizing that I, myself, had allowed my life to become unmanageable, I was able to ask and receive help in restoring myself to sanity with help from my Higher Power and help from my fellow-members.

The first time I really understood that I was my own worst enemy, that I was making my own difficulties, my mind began to stretch. It did not stretch all the way for quite a long time. I slipped back at times to self-pity and rebellion. But I did keep trying. The stretch reached just a little bit farther each time.

Now, with a perspective of long years between me and that old rebellious self, I can see I am a better person than before; it took all those upsets and heartbreaks to jolt me out of my complacency. Had I never had difficulties to surmount, I'd still be thinking of what was due me, not of what I should be doing to justify my being.

Life is a gift and an obligation. Unless we develop beyond the infant stage where we are wholly dependent upon what is done for us, without any thought of repayment, we are simply takers. We are living only a part of the life we were meant to live.

I was not happy through many of the drinking years. I can now see, however, that it took them to teach me my need of the Al-Anon program and my responsibility to those who need it now.

Al-Anon stretched my mind and it never can go back.

"Look for a Long Time"

LATELY I've been sad though I knew it was a "thing I cannot change." A line quoted by Robert Phelps in his preface to Colette's autobiography, Earthly Paradise, set me straight.

Colette, he says, once advised a young writer: "Look for a long time at what pleases you, and longer still at what pains you."

That bothered me considerably at first; it seemed totally against Al-Anon. Why couldn't I accept what had happened? But I couldn't.

My older brother was ill in Chicago with no hope of recovery but he could have lived months. Two urgent things kept me in New York: I had to finish March's FORUM and attend our quarterly Trustees' Board meeting. Then I took the first plane out.

I arrived to learn my brother had died in the night. Grateful as I was he hadn't suffered, thankful he'd known I was coming, I couldn't adjust myself to missing him by so little.

Death is always a shock, even when preceded by illness. All the past, a shared childhood, the growing up years and mutual joys and sorrows—those can't help but crowd one's mind and dim the sun when the one you spent them with is gone. I have adjusted to them in the past but what I could not endure was such a near miss.

When I read, "Look longer still at what pains you," I put the book down and went over everything in my mind in an inventory different from our Fourth Step but just as searching.

I found I was simply sorry for myself. Could I have said or done anything not already said or done for Jim? I saw I wasn't mourning for him but was sad because I'd missed him by so few hours. My grief was self-pity, reluctance to let go.

When I finally understood I was pitying myself, that it was me I was sorry for, I began to feel better. After all, those years and those joys are still in my mind. They live with me.

When I looked long enough I realized that missing Jim by half a day or half a year was not important. He is at rest and at peace, I am sure. He's had a good, useful life for the most part. Had he lived something might have developed which entailed suffering. Why should I ask more?

If you're sad, "Look long at what pleases you, and longer still at what pains you." It helps.

A "Tranquilizer" Highly Recommended

IN MARCH I spent a most rewarding weekend in Monroe, Louisiana, at the AA Birthday Party. Al-Anon had a place on the program and I flew down to speak. As always I had a wonderful time—Al-Anons and AAs are the most cordial, generous and appreciative audience one can find anywhere. They are more enthusiastic than children at a circus.

My flight home was via New Orleans, which I had never visited. At the last moment I changed my ticket so I could spend a day there, seeing a bit of that most interesting city.

Out at Lake Pontchartrain I learned hurricane warnings were up, which did little to make me anticipate my flight the next day. I've lived through two already and can't recommend them as good entertainment.

Next noon we took off in fairly decent weather which soon deteriorated until nothing could be seen from my window but the heaviest fog I've ever flown through.

About the time we were due to land at Kennedy airport, the stewardess announced we were coming in for a landing. I waited for hours for the NO SMOKING sign to come on.

Nothing happened.

Reports I'd read recently about planes hijacked and flown to Cuba inevitably came to mind. They'd included the detail that no announcement of a change in destination had been permitted, so that as time went on I became surer and surer we were headed for Havana and trouble.

If the fog was disturbing, that thought was worse. I had wondered before how long the Cubans were going to allow planes to land and take off without penalty; now my fervent hope was they hadn't changed their policy.

I'm not the worrywart I used to be but I cannot say I was wholly at my best. Then Al-Anon rescued me.

"Can I stop this fog? Can I do one single thing about where we're going to put down? We are seven miles up above the earth—what can I do about it?" Answers were unanimously negative. Wasn't this, then, "a thing I couldn't change?"

"Where is your Al-Anon?" I asked myself. "You travel thousands of miles to tell your experience in Al-Anon, hoping to help someone else. How can you possibly expect to be anything but a tinkling cymbal or sounding brass if YOU don't practice the program yourself. Better pull up your socks and get at it."

It took no wisdom to know I was in a situation I couldn't change, so no courage was involved in needlessly trying to change it. The only thing left was to seek serenity to accept whatever eventuated. I just concentrated on that: "I am in God's hands. His will, not mine, be done. Live as you'd like to die, in trust and hope, and not in craven fear."

So I stopped gluing my eyes to my watch and went back to reading my paperback murder. An hour or so later the stewardess announced that we were above Kennedy and would "hold" for forty-five minutes while other planes landed ahead of us.

Little as I like "holding" at any time, in a blinding fog I hate it. But by then I had enough serenity to realize immediately I was powerless in this situation too. Again I returned to my mystery and read another hour until we put down in a cloudburst. I thanked God and gratefully got off.

Next morning my *Times* carried an account of another plane which was hijacked to Cuba the day before!

Later I had a lovely note from Monroe, thanking me for my talk, in which Theresa told me someone had said at their meeting, "If Margaret had flown today, she might have been on that plane—think of it!"

"I said," wrote Theresa, "if she had been, she'd probably just do a piece in the FORUM about it." How right she was and how well she knew me! I was in the midst of writing this very article when her note came and I hadn't even been hijacked. I laugh every time I think of it.

But what it all amounts to is that for someone who had such initial and prolonged difficulty in getting our program, I have to concentrate on it constantly and keep on "practicing it in ALL my affairs."

Should any of you find yourself seven miles above the earth, in a blinding fog, I cannot recommend too highly asking to be granted "the serenity to accept the things you cannot change" and to "Let Go and Let God."

Don't Let It Throw You

NOTHING I HAVE ever heard or read indicated that life was meant to be one sweet song after another. No one promised there'd never be a discordant note nor a major disappointment.

But all too often such happenings occur. When they do, many of us catch ourselves thinking that life is more difficult today then ever before. Is it?

Job had enough set-backs for a regiment. His unshaken

belief, "Blessed is the man whom God correcteth" was enough to keep him going. He lived through all afflictions and was rewarded greatly.

When General Anthony C. McAuliffe, trapped for a week at Bastogne in the Battle of the Bulge, was presented with an ultimatum from the Germans, demanding he surrender the remnants of his 101st Airborne Division, he kept up his courage, and that of all his men, with his off-hand and contemptuous "Nuts."

These are extreme examples of life's hazards. Few of us are likely to find ourselves in such desperate circumstances. But are we meeting much lesser ills with like acceptance? How often do we quail before really minor difficulties?

We set ourselves a goal, even work diligently toward reaching it. When we fail, fall short of accomplishing all of it, all too often we say, "I can't do that. It's too hard for me."

Maybe we did fail at first. But that shouldn't throw us. Perhaps our aim was set too high for the time being. Rather than abandon that goal, it would be better for us to put it aside for a while and attack it a bit later, when we are more prepared, have more knowledge.

All of us have seen newcomers come to Al-Anon, filled with enthusiasm for the program. They eagerly accept what they are told, and are overjoyed if their partners go into AA. But let misfortune come and that partner un-happily has a slip, they abandon everything and say to themselves, "Why should I continue in Al-Anon if George is going to drink?" So they leave the group.

It does little good to remind these people that we work at this program to get help for ourselves, not to sober up our spouses. They have been completely thrown by the first adversity.

If they would refuse to be thus thrown, if they'd pick

themselves up after just a little stumble, attack the program anew, listen with more open minds and apply what they hear, most likely they'd achieve success. At least their own lives would be more tranquil.

Queerly enough, by reaching that enviable state, their partners often are inspired to reach it too. Success almost inevitably crowns the efforts of those who refuse to be thrown.

Giving up is easy enough. But it almost always leads to more trouble. When disaster comes, or even just minor disappointment, say to yourself, "Don't let it throw me." Give yourself a rest and begin over again.

Through Other Eyes

PROUST HAS ALWAYS seemed beyond my powers of concentration so that I've never really disciplined myself to take on his "Remembrance of Things Past." But a quotation I came upon recently delighted me.

It said, in effect, it would do us little good to grow wings and to develop different breathing so that we could voyage into space, if our own senses remained unchanged.

According to Proust a voyage of discovery would be possible only if we looked through "other eyes, to behold the universe through the eyes of another, of a hundred others, to behold the hundred universes that each of them beholds, that each of them is."

This enchanted me. It instantly brought back a summer day, several years ago, when I sat and watched one of my favorite grandsons (I have two!) make a candy house which absorbed and delighted him.

He had cut the ends of a small carton into triangles to

form peaks and had fitted cardboard over them to make a roof. He'd glued graham crackers, smeared sketchily with a white frosting, to cover the house's sides and was busy dipping gum-drops into egg white to make them stick to the roof.

He frowned when he saw that only a few gum-drops were left, while half the roof was still bare. "Honey," I said, "those gum-drops are flat, top and bottom. I think if you'd make three slices of them, they would cover the roof."

Happily the idea worked, even though the effect of bumpy, whole gum-drops and flat slices of them was on the bizarre side. To his six-year-old eyes, it was obviously beautiful.

My daughter joined us for a moment and afterwards said, "Mommie, you were completely absorbed by Billy's house. What were you thinking about?" "I was just thinking that I'd give a million to be able to see that house through Billy's eyes," I answered—and then forgot it.

My daughter is an elephant for memory; she really listens and never forgets. Months later she reminded me of it; told me she hadn't been able to get it out of her mind. Every time she became impatient, trying to understand something silly Billy had done, she had remembered my wish to see his house through his eyes, and had relaxed.

Those few words of Proust brought all this back—made me realize that if we judge and value everything about us only by our own experience and standards, we don't really grow or develop.

But if we bother "to look through the eyes of another," a whole new world can reveal itself to us, even in our everyday surroundings. Fifteen minutes of such looking could do more for us, I believe, mentally and spiritually, than any other exercise.

Try looking through the eyes of another and see what you discover.

"When You Can't Do as You Would . . ."

THE LAST PLACE in the world one would expect to come upon Al-Anon philosophy is in a gardening book, published almost a hundred years ago. But there it was, waiting for me to find it.

I read it because I admired the spunky author, not because of need for the gardening lore in it. We live in an aerie overlooking the Hudson, a sixteenth floor apartment with not even a windowbox. The only plants we have are lilies at Easter, poinsettias at Christmas and a pot of chives which die every time we go away.

"Gardening by Myself" was written by Anna B. Warner in 1872 when she was past fifty. She and her sister lived alone on Constitution Island, opposite West Point, in very straitened circumstances after having enjoyed great wealth. She wrote twenty books and collaborated with her sister Susan on nineteen more, many of them best-sellers in their day.

An avid gardener, Anna's great love was a profusion of flowers. Winter nights she pored over catalogues and planned how best to spend the little money she could spare for seeds.

She never regretted her inability to afford the expensive new offerings, although she read every glowing word about them. She simply looked forward to the day when she could buy them. As she wrote, "What I can afford must come even before what I want," and the price of one seed of an untried novelty would buy packets of five to ten reliable old favorites. I was glad to read that she did occasionally plunge, on a less expensive new seed.

She wrote that gardeners frowned upon planting seeds in pots instead of in professional flats. She did not have flats and could neither afford them nor build them herself. Thus she made do—quite successfully, too—with pots. "When you can't do as you would," she wrote, "you must do as you can."

After Susan's death when Anna was sixty-five, she lived quite alone on the island for thirty years until her death in 1915. If anyone commented upon her solitary life she always said, "I am not alone; God is with me."

On almost every page of her little book there is some reflection of the acceptance and serenity we strive for in Al-Anon. She never looked back in regret and she never looked forward with anxiety.

I think of her many times when I hear someone at a meeting castigating herself for something done in the past. One woman I know cannot forgive herself for hospitalizing her husband, because he resented it so greatly. I feel it was all she could do at the time: he had the entire family in such fear and uproar they had to be protected temporarily. I agree with Miss Anna, "When you can't do as you would, you must do as you can."

Few, if any, of us live lives of such perfect acceptance as Miss Anna did. She had no need of Al-Anon; apparently she was born with the whole program at her fingertips.

We are different. We do need it. And, through Al-Anon, we can follow in her footsteps, daily to come nearer our goal of serenity.

What Do You Want?

"THE MOST frightening people are those who do not know what they want; we therefore must devote all our energy to the business of making our wishes completely clear." Maxim Gorky.

Anyone who has lived through a hurricane remembers it for an experience he would not like repeated. Yet, pre-Al-Anon, many of us were violently blown about by storms at home, yet always went back for repeat performances.

Many wished we had never met our partners and thus would have escaped present circumstances. Or many wished we had recognized the situation before children arrived. And many more wished for an end, any end, to the mess in which we lived. Only a blind sense of responsibility or habit had made us remain with an alcoholic partner.

The truth is that we really didn't know what we wanted, that we were frightened, vacillating people. In our confusion we simply felt that if the drinking partner stopped drinking, everything would be all right.

Then came the Al-Anon program to set us straight, to give us goals and purpose. It taught us that what happens to a person is not nearly so important as what we do about the happening, how we meet whatever comes with it.

When the Al-Anon program showed us a goal of serenity and acceptance amid whatever confusion existed, we stopped being helplessly tossed about. We stopped our childish rebellion which expressed itself in transitory dreams of escape. We stopped being potential time-bombs, ready to explode upon any provocation.

When Al-Anon centered our desires upon an ordered, meaningful life, and showed us how to attain it, we at last began to mature, to become useful, valuable as human beings, instead of frightened, frightening, haunted spirits.

Deciding what we want to be, and bending every effort toward making ourselves as near to that person as possible, is our main purpose in Al-Anon. It can, and in fact has, changed the lives of thousands.

176

One Day's FORUM Mail

IF IT WERE possible to reward each good letter, item or idea sent to the FORUM, I believe the best award possible would be to have the contributor of it sit at my desk for a day.

You all know by now the joy I have in editing the FORUM. Many of you have heard me say I wouldn't change places even with Lois, who really got Al-Anon going, when she and Anne first began work on a few names given them by the AA General Office. Bless them both, because I edit the FORUM as a result of their work.

Never-ending, always fascinating, dovetailing of experience, inspiration, joy in success, courage in adverse circumstances, generosity of spirit—all these are shared in letters to the FORUM. Reading them and putting them together is like working out a jig-saw puzzle.

This piece goes here; it came from South Dakota. That piece which came from New Zealand, goes next it, and a third from France, perhaps, fits above both. A whole friendly world spreads itself before me.

Take Adele's letter from Las Vegas, Nevada, in this FORUM. She, with Al-Anon's help, had learned acceptance, had realized that a compelling drive for impossible perfection could ruin her life.

At the same time, Teresa R., our WSD from Tennessee, sent in a wonderful bit she'd heard at an AA meeting; the speaker said he "had attained peace of mind somewhere between his ambitions and his limitations."

If those two letters do not belong together, neither do bread and butter. And they are of prime importance to all of us. They have a large part of our program wrapped up in them.

Too many of us set ourselves impossible goals. We perhaps try to do too much too soon. If we accomplish even half what we aim at, we may well be doing more than could really be expected of us. But because we did not attain everything we wanted, we feel we failed.

No one likes to live with failure, so we become discouraged. We may go so far wrong through discouragement, as to stop trying. Right here Adele's acceptance, and Teresa's AA speaker, have our answer: absolute perfection is beyond any of us. Peace of mind comes from a realistic appraisal of our ambitions, goals, limitations and accomplishments.

Each of us has his own job to do in life. Someone else might be able to do it better. But he is probably having a struggle to do his own job the best way he can.

I probably can do my grandson's spelling lessons to the Queen's taste, in no time flat and with no effort. But I'm an adult who has spent a lifetime learning, and he's a little boy, just at the beginning. I sometimes have problems in my own life and work, which are just as difficult for me.

The main point, as I see it, is to begin SOMEWHERE and KEEP AT IT. We have much to help us in our program. "Just For Today," "Take It Easy," the Serenity Prayer, and above all, innumerable accounts at meetings which testify to what Al-Anon has done to make countless lives happy again. All these are ours, just for the effort of listening, and practicing them.

Our main goal is serenity and peace of mind. If others have succeeded in reaching them, we can, too. And if I never can reward those writers of the most helpful messages, I need not upset myself. I can always print the letters!

Merry Christmas to Al-Anons and Alateens

MY DEARS:

Again my wish for you this year is like last year's: "May every Christmas joy be yours and may Al-Anon strengthen and guide you all through the year."

Twelve months have passed since that was written. In the same article I said that Christmas is not only a day but a time and feeling, that we cannot let our program be a one-day anniversary, that we need to "get it and give it" every day in some way. It's a good habit to establish.

Now, near the end of this old year and the beginning of a new one, it seems appropriate that we all review what was accomplished in 1968. Some of you accepted responsibility for group leadership, which surely contributed to Al-Anon's effectiveness. Others did much excellent Twelfth Step work, which increased Al-Anon's growth. Others made strides in personal understanding and practice of the program, which made them more valuable members.

You can look back with satisfaction on having done any or all of these things. But one fascinating and stimulating part of Al-Anon work is that you can bring new life and hope to someone in trouble or despair without realizing it. It sometimes is many months, even years, later that you learn you did help and how you did it.

Perhaps there's a letter in the FORUM which tells of new insight gained from a letter printed months before. You glow all over when you realize that that first letter was your own contribution. Perhaps just one person wrote in gratitude for the first letter; it's very possible, however, dozens of others got the same lift from it but didn't write.

Sometimes when you've given a talk at another group, and a year or so later when you meet a member of it, he tells that what you said in your talk enlightened him and spurred him on.

Again, you may make a brief comment at your own meeting and not know until much later that what you said was the first chink in a defensive member's armor, or a tightly closed mind until that moment, which led to his acceptance of the program.

When I think of this unknown reservoir of Al-Anon inspiration, it always reminds me of the early days at the Clearing House. Some days mail was heavy; forty or fifty letters answering cries for help were written and mailed. Occasionally there were only ten or a dozen. Lois invariably commented, as we prepared to go home, "Well, we got a lot done today, didn't we!"

We, just as invariably, teased her about her standard comment on our efforts. But all she'd do was smile her lovely, reasuring smile, and repeat, "We did get a lot done."

And the queer part is that she probably was exactly right. There was no way to tell which of the days did the most good. But there is utterly no question at all but that Lois' encouragement always helped, always inspired us to work a bit harder and to feel the great importance of that work. We felt wonderful.

So, in looking back over 1968, if you wish you had done more Twelfth Step work, had accepted a group office or any other responsibility you think you perhaps skimped on, remember Lois: you very likely got a lot done, a great part of which you may never know about.

And there's always 1969, in which you can work harder.

Love and happy holidays to you.

"Even the Desert Blooms"

EVERYONE WHO KNOWS Lois knows her passionate love of flowers, plants, trees and everything to do with gardens. *Stepping Stones* well repays her tireless work in its beauty, simplicity and tranquility.

Thus it was not accidental that the analogy of working in a garden and working the Al-Anon program came to her when she wrote "BEFORE AL-ANON . . . Loneliness and Despair."

Over the years I have read it many times—back in the old days of the Clearing House (when it was titled "One Wife's Story), it was one of the only three pieces of literature we had. But then, as now, it did yeoman work for those who took the quarter-hour's time to read it.

Each time I read it, some new idea comes to me, something fresh and encouraging emerges to inspire me.

Reading it today, where she writes of different soils and how flowers can be grown in each, I found, "Even the desert blooms." Probably I've heard that sentence thirty or forty times. But only today did I realize the wisdom and comfort of it.

It impressed me now particularly because I've been thinking so constantly about a member of my group. She has hit a bad patch in recent weeks and in spite of a previous fine grasp and practice of Al-Anon principles, she finds herself depressed, questioning what she is putting into and getting out of Al-Anon.

As I listened to her, I knew she was totally unlike her usual self. As I heard her quickly sketch her recent activities, I knew why: she was tired to the bone but had been forcing herself to carry on as usual.

It was no wonder to me that something gave—something

had to: the stoutest of spirits occasionally flag. But when I read, "Even the desert blooms," I knew I had found comfort for my discouraged friend.

Think for a moment what that means. I've never seen a desert, in or out of bloom, just splendid pictures in the magazine, "Arizona Highways" which show a profusion of beautiful flowers, springing out of endless wastes of sand.

And remembering those glorious pictures, it came to me that we, too, have desert-places in our lives, just as my fellow-member has right now.

We don't know when our deserts will bloom, when the arid stretches will blossom into beauty. But we do know that as long as we are alive there is hope; trite but very true.

It may well be that we sometimes need these low spots in our lives; we cannot live at the peak always. As the desert needs rest and quiescence before it flames into bloom, just so may we need dormant periods to enable us to reach greater heights of understanding and acceptance.

If "Even the desert blooms," so can we. So can my dear friend.

Who Would Want to Be Infallible?

ONE OF THE GREATEST things about Al-Anon is the universality and common sense of its philosophy. One bit or another is almost sure-fire to straighten out any situation.

Take the Steps for instance. No one says they are easy to follow nor to be swallowed in one gulp. But, if you work at them conscientiously, give them due thought and make them an integral part of your life, you will be well-armed to face difficulties.

They teach you to work toward perfection, instead of assuming that you are perfect to begin with and have fallen into error through human perversity.

The Tenth Step is a good illustration. "Continued to take personal inventory and when we were wrong promptly admitted it." This Step does not say we have failed, even if we *have* failed miserably by making mistakes. It assumes that everyone does make mistakes occasionally and it implies that we begin to correct errors by recognizing them as such and by admitting them promptly.

All this was summed up quite succinctly for me the other day when I ran across a quotation—unfortunately the source wasn't given so I can't give credit. However the quote is a honey:

"The great may go wrong but they do not try to cover their tracks."

Could anything be more simple? Or more in keeping with the Al-Anon program? Or more comforting? It seems to say to you, "Surely the great are great, but even great people make mistakes. The only thing is that they don't ignore them, don't try to pretend they didn't make any."

Fortunately I live in a very normal family of human beings and I cannot think of any winged angels among them. I'm right at home with them and among my peers when I go wrong. Were they all perfect I'm sure I'd long since have been read out of the family and I believe I'd be as well content not to have to compete with absolute perfection!

The thing I have to remember is that I frequently do wrong things but that I can help to minimize those failings by admitting them, by not trying to pretend they never happened by covering them up.

That takes us straight back to Al-Anon's Tenth Step of

promptly admitting wrongs. It's certainly easier to blame another person, to think that he very likely provoked us into loss of control but it's not Al-Anon.

And when you think it all over, it seems to me it's a lot better to begin a little lower down and to rise higher through your own efforts than it is to start at the top and slide down through your own faults.

I don't believe I'd have lived this long, in my particular setting, if I were smugly perfect, infallibly right. No one could bear to have me around—they'd probably have extinguished me long since. And I could well understand that!

Always Tend to Your Own Knitting

MORE THAN a hundred years ago, in "Walden," Henry D. Thoreau wrote: "The mass of men lead lives of quiet desperation." Without doubt he was a true eccentric but his injunction, again in "Walden," to "Beware of all enterprises that require new clothes," always had endeared him to me and gave weight to what he wrote. I couldn't believe anyone who loved old clothes, as I do myself, could be very wrong.

On the principle that misery loves company, for many years I comforted myself with the thought that, indeed, most men do lead lives of quiet desperation. I was not unique, although my desperation was not always quiet.

Al-Anon's philosophy and program, when I really studied it deeply and accepted it, showed me that even so discerning a thinker as Thoreau could be wrong or at least hadn't thought far enough. I learned that there was no need and no excuse for desperation, quiet or otherwise.

I came to believe desperation stems from not being able to do anything constructive in a serious situation. Without Al-Anon's Family Group program I could only rebel futilely.

The thing which had driven me frantic was that I could see no good in and no excuse for the excessive and uncontrolled drinking. It upset our family relationships; played havoc with our finances, kept me on tenterhooks whether my husband was drinking or not and worst of all, he didn't even enjoy it!

I believe that last thought was what offended me most. My Scot's blood, generations back though it is, protested the extravagant waste of it. I really believe I could have borne it better, and suffered less, had he derived any pleasure from it.

You can see how far I was from realizing there was any compulsion about an alcoholic's drinking. Al-Anon, although it took me a long time to get it, did teach and help me.

I came to accept the fact of alcoholism as a disease, which only my husband could control. I came to believe that my part in our lives was to accept my own powerlessness over alcohol. Al-Anon taught me to concentrate my efforts on regaining my own serenity and making our family life as tranquil as I could.

Thoreau went on to say that "what is called resignation is confirmed desperation." I believe this. People say you should resign yourself to what you cannot change. Webster defines resign as surrender, quit, abandon, relinquish. All these are negative ideas, which I couldn't accomplish, so I did become desperate.

Al-Anon says, "Accept the things I cannot change." It was only with this acceptance that I began to come up, for what was practically the third time.

By accepting powerlessness, by admitting what was my own role and my own province, the desperation lessened and finally disappeared. Al-Anon taught me to tend to my own knitting and leave my husband to tend to his.

Serenity: Our Greatest Safeguard

"WHEN I FEEL the calm of my spirit has been broken by emotional upset, then I must steal away alone . . ." because "uncalm times are the only times when evil can find an entrance."

This is from a book my AA husband is so devoted to that he reads to me from it and we have what amounts to a short, private meeting.

This business of uncalm times leading to the entrance of evil seemed particularly apt to me because of a worrying situation in which I am at present involved. The emphasis on serenity in our program has always been, to me, one of the greatest values of all.

When I came to Al-Anon I was thoroughly sick and tired of the turmoil I had created for years within myself. I desperately wanted the serenity I saw in my fellow members but somehow could not acknowledge my powerlessness over alcohol. Always there was that stubborn hope I would somehow think up the perfect gimmick to entice my husband into sobriety. Only when it finally penetrated my resistant mind exactly where my responsibility—or capability—ended and his began, did I appreciate the futility of batting my spirit against something I could not change. Only then did a measure of serenity come and was reflected in our household. A truly blessed day!

At present I can see much of my old self in two wives,

both of whom I met through AA; one is in Al-Anon, the other not. Except that I never sought outside help, that I kept all my anger, resentment and despair at a rolling boil within myself, these two women are at present as unable to help themselves and their mates as I was. They keep trying, though, however misguidedly.

So far as I can tell, both husbands are making valiant efforts toward sobriety under difficult circumstances. And what circumstances aren't difficult in this problem? Tensions would certainly be lessened if the wives could somehow really practice the Serenity Prayer.

Instead, despite some months of abstinence by both spouses, if either is late ten minutes in arriving home, the wife immediately thinks the worst and is visibly upset when her husband gets home. Both are breath-sniffers, although what either could do if she got a whiff is beyond me.

Neither wife seems ever to relax; their phones are constantly busy with calls to friends, where complaints of past binges, fear of one beginning soon and dread of future ones is their main topic. It is all but impossible to get a word in.

None of this is good. Even the non-Al-Anon wife has been told enough of our program by now to know she is adding gigantic hazards to steady sobriety. Why, then, do they continue in so fruitless an effort?

They have, I believe, worked themselves into such a frenzy that they now cannot stop by themselves. Their "wrongs" occupy so large a part of their minds they can no longer listen to what is said—they just wait until the speaker pauses and then take up where they left off.

Do I believe either situation is hopeless, even though it sometimes surely seems so? No, I decidedly do not. Disheartening, yes; discouraging, yes, but hopeless, no. Too many miracles have occurred in Al-Anon and AA for me ever to despair of new ones. Sometime, some word most likely will open a crack in deaf ears. Some day an unexpected chink will let a small ray of light into the darkest place. And peace will come to them and to their husbands.

These are extreme cases. They developed from fear, upset and emotional uncontrol into practically major catastrophes. The only good I can see in either is that others of us may learn object lessons from them.

The very moment we feel "the calm of our spirit broken by emotional upset," that very moment we must make ourselves aware that evil can enter and we should steal away alone to regain serenity.

No Problem Is Without a Solution

A LETTER to the FORUM told of a problem a member found most disturbing. It didn't seem an insurmountable situation to us at all. But it did to the writer.

Esther B., Montclair, N.J., of the Editorial Board, commented in discussing it, "A very wise doctor said to me once that if something is a problem to you, it IS a problem and must be solved. Do not compare your problems with those of others."

That observation has recurred to me a dozen times since Esther tossed it out so lightly. In fact, I believe it is as good as a whole meeting if we just apply it thoughtfully.

It took me back to the most frustrating year of my life, out on the beautiful Montana ranch I had hoped to keep operating while my husband was with the 14th Air Force in China. I felt a great responsibility to him and to his partner. I also considered my running the ranch my special contribution to WW II: food production was vital; the country needed beef, pigs, turkeys, hay and grain.

The season was late; everything took longer to do because it was impossible to get adequate help—the hay crew was four, instead of a dozen. Grain was so late maturing there was great danger it would freeze as it stood.

I read government bulletins by lamplight, late into the night; I talked to the most successful ranchers in the valley to learn their shortcuts. They were generous in telling me how things should be best done under the circumstances. I would tactfully and confidently tell my "boys" how we could save time and work by doing what the J Bar L was going to do.

They would agree. But time after time they held to the way they and their fathers had done things in Nebraska, under very different circumstances. They privately agreed no fool woman's newfangled notions would change them.

Had I had Al-Anon's teaching then, I'd have accepted it as a thing I couldn't change, which is the solution I finally found. I was a little ashamed of it then. Many times I walked the floor in desperation; took my .22 to a pasture gophers were ruining and tried to wipe them out; many times I just sat sadly on a stump and looked at the mountains.

It was a very real problem. It did no good to get furious with them, to remind myself they had promised Jack they'd work for me as they would for him while he went to war. I wasn't happy with the solution but I'm sure now it was the only one in an impossible situation.

Very much earlier, at eight or nine, I'd found a satisfactory solution to a very important problem: I had been fitted for glasses and hated them. They were ruining my life, I thought. In less than two weeks I broke them three times. I'd take them to my father and say, quite truthfully,

"I broke my glasses." Since I played with boys a lot, Father probably thought it natural I'd have more difficulties with my glasses than my quiet older sister. He'd get them repaired.

Breaking the glasses solved nothing; they just got mended, so I put my mind on the problem: I went out to a large marshy place, shut my eyes, whirled them around my head and let go. That night, when asked where they were, I said, again truthfully if deceitfully, "I don't know—they're lost."

With that my father gave up. I'm sure I couldn't have needed them badly as it wasn't until college, when horn-rims were fashionable, that I asked for some. Very likely there was a better solution than the one I found but I did find a solution.

In Al-Anon my greatest problem was the First Step. I fought it for years and years, thus complicating the whole problem for myself and my family. I knew others accepted it almost immediately but it continued to be a problem to me.

Then, after years, in what I'm sure was a spiritual awakening, it suddenly flashed upon me that I actually WAS powerless over alcohol. That made sense and that problem was solved.

So, if you have a problem, big or small, think it through until you find the solution you can accept. Don't panic. Don't think in circles. When you find yourself protesting against the problem, haul your mind off the protest and put it back to hunting for a sensible solution.

There's always one if you look hard enough.

Use Al-Anon's Armor to Combat Useless Fear

FEAR UNDOUBTEDLY has its uses: children must be taught to fear strange bottles lest they swallow poison. Fear drives us to seek help from competent doctors lest we develop serious disorders. Fear is sometimes a valuable warning device. But also it frequently is a rot, as the poet Robert Graves says.

This kind of fear, this rot, is the kind which harms so many in our fellowship. They come to groups so fear-ridden they cannot, at first, accept the offered enlightenment. They are so steeped in apprehensions they cannot listen attentively. Their minds continually stray and jump from one anxiety to another, more dire than the first.

Years ago, someone sent the FORUM a wonderful Stopper: "Fear knocked at the door. Faith answered. And lo, there was no one there!" It has been quoted in several of my articles since then. Many members have re-submitted it, not knowing or remembering it had already been printed. But with Al-Anon's constantly increasing membership, this stimulating little precept, admonition, exhortation—call it what you will—merits as frequent repetition as the Serenity Prayer.

So much of Al-Anon's philosophy is packed into those short sentences—so easily remembered—that they constantly come to mind when I'm doing Twelfth Step work.

Fear has knocked at so many of our doors, both before and after we first came to Al-Anon, there's little need to expand the point. We actually lived in a welter of fears, big and small, unable to cope with them.

Gradually, as Al-Anon's teachings began to penetrate our fog, we gained a little hope and an assurance that things could probably never be half as bad as we feared.

We gained enough faith actually to examine our fears and to face them.

When we did face them, we realized that many were bogeymen, figments of our own imaginations. Frequently they never materialized. Many of Al-Anon's slogans bear on this subject:

• Easy Does It—don't knock yourself out, fearing what probably isn't there.

• Let Go and Let God—you can't have everything to suit yourself but never fear, your Higher Power will help you cope.

• Twenty-four Hours a Day—concentrate on just this moment and not on the fear of what might, but hasn't yet, happened.

• First Things First—you can never gain the serenity you seek if you dissipate your strength in nameless fears.

• Live and Let Live—your life is too important to you and to others for you to spend it in a turmoil of fear. Live it confidently and don't penalize those around you by making them live with a craven shell of yourself.

"Fear knocked at the door. Faith answered. And lo, there was no one there!" There's a lot of meaning packed into those few words. You'll find new meanings every time you give them a little thought. They are a very valuable part of Al-Anon's arsenal against slips.

Al-Anon's Program Enlightens the World

STRAY GLIMPSES of long-familiar sights sometimes have a most unusual effect. They stimulate new insights, give new inspiration, new determination to try harder to do a job which occasionally has become routine.

A sketch of the Statue of Liberty jolted me recently. I've seen her dozens of times, from the deck of a ship and from the air. From the air she's never been particularly impressive—just a sort of identification I'm on my way West somewhere.

But from shipboard there's always been a catch in my throat, a wonderment of what she must mean to the thousands of immigrants who see her as evidence of a dream come true.

The drawing was just part of an ad, with a quote from the poem on the pedestal: "Give me your tired, your poor, your huddled masses yearning to breathe free . . . Send these . . . to me: I lift my lamp beside the golden door."

As I looked at the sketch I suddenly felt it was Al-Anon standing there, instead of a woman with a crown on her head, a torch in one hand, a book in the other. I saw a different symbolism in it. I saw the spirit of Al-Anon going out to the whole world, ready and eager to share its blessings of healing, hope and knowledge with anyone in need.

Not everyone who enters Liberty's golden door finds a perfect life. Perhaps some seek an unreasonable dream. But surely no one ever sought in vain, for relief from intolerable burdens, in Al-Anon, if he honestly tried to follow its precepts. It is perfectly true that not all who come to Al-Anon stay with it. Occasionally even established members drop out.

In such cases, it seems to me, there is an unwillingness to give up, an inability to keep an open mind, a rejection of some important part of the program which accounts for the failure.

"Principles above personalities" is difficult for those who have always allowed themselves to indulge in personal likes and dislikes in judging actions. Some find it difficult to subordinate themselves and their wishes to the common good of the Al-Anon group. Some are content to listen, more or less perfunctorily, to Al-Anon's teachings and leave it at that.

But to those who are eager to know and to understand exactly how and why they should change old ways, Al-Anon's lamp can shine through any door. We all were tired, poor. We huddled, not in masses usually, but miserably within ourselves. Above all, we yearned to "breathe free." In desperation we came to Al-Anon.

Many of us found there a ray of hope when we learned that an illness, not wanton self-indulgence, willfulness nor shameful selfishness caused the situation which made us so unhappy. We began to realize our responsibility for our share in making that situation worse. We learned that even if we could not change the situation, we could accept it and live with it.

Once our own burden has been lifted or lightened by the gifts Al-Anon has bestowed, in return for our following its program, we are able to "breathe free." We are able to think of others and, above everything else, to share those gifts with others who still live in the darkness which once encompassed us.

Al-Anon must be boundless while there is one case of alcoholism still not arrested. Part of its glory is the inspiration it gives most of us to share its blessings. Passing on to others the benefits we have ourselves gained is our repayment for restored hope and happiness.

Twelfth Step work is, and should be, endless.

Al-Anon is Not a Sometime Thing

PEOPLE OFTEN ASK me why long-timers remain in our program. Surely, they say, after 15 to 20 years, there can't be much that is new in it for them—much to be learned about it.

194

The basics of the program are said to be very simple. They probably could be learned in a few meetings: alcoholism is an incurable illness and is primarily the alcoholic's business; we have no control over alcohol; our responsibility and our field of endeavor is within ourselves and with families of alcoholics; we can attain serenity even though the problem remains active; we can learn to live with dignity and quiet content, without letting alcoholic excess overwhelm us; we have just today in which to work; our goal is spiritual growth through the constant practice of the Twelve Steps; our obligation to the Al-Anon Family Groups is through a thorough understanding and faithful practice of the Twelve Traditions. There may even be something I have skipped in this quick summing up.

Now there may be some people who can master these "simple" principles, once and for all. But if so, I definitely am not among them.

It's true that in grade school arithmetic I once learned the multiplication tables—at least up to the "nine times . . ." table. I'm still unreliable there. And please don't tell me they're the easiest as the product always adds up to nine itself; that just adds another confusion factor for me. I still know those tables cold. But the Al-Anon program is entirely different.

Just take the Steps and the Serenity Prayer, for instance. I need to work on them constantly. The First Step and the first sentence of the Prayer are like Siamese Twins: inseparably joined, as far as I am concerned. They are connected, not just with alcohol but with many other situations in which I find myself. I need to examine each hurdle as it comes along to see if it is something over which I am powerless or if it is something I can change. I also need to gauge whether it could make my life unmanageable.

The decision to let God's will prevail is another fertile field for constant work. And the practice of these principles in all my affairs is not like learning multiplication tables. Without the constant reminders of active Al-Anon work I'm sure I'd honor a lot of them more "in the breach than the observance."

I don't believe I'm overly stupid nor self-willed. But I do believe I need frequent nudges. I get them from our Al-Anon program.

No human life has ever been perfect but Al-Anon can show me how to profit from the imperfections, rather than wasting time and energy in damaging resentments. Others may not need this reminder. But I do.

It is possible that some people have minds which are stocked and stored with all manner of information and resources, neatly assorted like books on library shelves.

Perhaps if I knew some of those people the temptation to abolish them would be strong, because my mind is a hodge-podge of assorted ideas based upon appealing bits picked up from here, there and everywhere. I never quite know what stimulus is going to set something boiling up, what bit will float to the surface from the disorderly depths.

But I've lived with that disorder a long time. I've constantly added new gems to it. And Al-Anon helps me haul them out when I need them. No one should ever "graduate" from Al-Anon. I'm afraid that if I ever tried to graduate myself from the program, everything would sink into a useless mess.

The shiningest bits I've added in the past 17 or 18 years have come, almost in toto, from Al-Anon. Take Barbara T's letter about resentments in this month's Answering Service. If I had graduated myself a month or two ago, I'd never have known the fundamental reason why I always pray immediately for someone who has hurt or annoyed me.

I've done it usually to get my mind off the hurt. But I now understand from her letter that it comes from an unconscious recognition of brotherhood. If any utter stranger provoked me, I'd brush it off instinctively. But as Barbara wrote, "God loves him just as much as He does me, is in him as much as in me," so I toss off a quick prayer for someone who is really my brother and feel calm again.

The more I think of what Al-Anon does for everyone who is wise enough to follow the program, the less I understand anyone dropping out or neglecting it. To me, it's a chance-of-a-lifetime, for-a-lifetime philosophy.

Al-Anons are Modern Alchemists

AL-ANON Twelfth Step work sometimes does not seem as dramatic as that of AA. I look among our friends and see men whom my husband Twelfth Stepped twenty, ten, five or three years ago. When I think they have not had a drink in all those years I occasionally wonder how my Al-Anon work stacks up beside his. And that is daft. There are far better ways for me to spend my time.

Al-Anon Twelfth Step work is quite as essential as that of AA. If that of AA successfully brings sobriety to the alcoholic, that of Al-Anon restores mental sobriety to whole families. Even though they had not been physically drunk, most of their lives had been as greatly out of control and as unmanageable as though they too had suffered from the disease of alcoholism.

Changes usually come more slowly in Al-Anon than in AA and, as said before, they don't seem as dramatic. When a drunk stops drinking, when he wholeheartedly accepts AA, he stops a lot of other things which used to make him stand out from his fellowmen. Even those who had been uncontrolled drinkers for twenty or thirty years seem able to take up life again with confidence and courage.

Courage, I believe, returns more slowly to the non-alcoholic partners. Perhaps because they have for so long a time built their lives and their outlook around their alcoholic mates—have been happy when there was a break in the drinking, sad when it was renewed—they now fear to believe that sobriety will endure.

However they do at last realize they do not control, and never have controlled, the alcoholic problem. They learn to put that problem back into the hands where it always had belonged: the Higher Power's and the alcoholic's. But to overcome their edginess, mistrust and inability to relax requires considerable time.

With Al-Anon's help they regain the ability to relax. They lose their mistrust and edginess little by little. They begin to enjoy life anew, rejoin the human race they have shut out for so long. They take up relationships and occupations long abandoned.

Fairly soon they learn to recognize in newcomers the need they themselves once suffered. They know what needs to be done and they are able to stretch out their willing hands to do it.

Let no one say that "the years of the locust" were extravagantly wasted ones, as I once considered them. Alchemists of the Middle Ages spent their whole lives futilely trying to turn base metals into gold. But through Al-Anon we have learned how to turn the dross of unhappy, rebellious years into the living gold of happiness, peace, serenity and hope . . . not just for ourselves but for all who seek help.

Speak to Newcomers in Their Own Language

ONE OF Al-Anon's greatest strengths is the ability to identify properly with fellow members. And it is not a "misery-
loves-company" sort of thing, either.

All but a fortunate few come to their first meeting in
desperation. Suffering under the old idea that excessive
drinking was a disgrace, ignorant that it is an illness, most
newcomers have imprisoned themselves behind high,
strong walls which not only shut them in but keep all
others out. They are their own jailers.

Families, friends and neighbors were kept at arm's length
lest they stumble upon what we considered our "shameful
secret." Some of these newcomers, it is true, had cast dignity to the winds and everlastingly complained about their
suffering to anyone who'd listen. They had not realized
that understanding was needed, not the weakening sym-
pathy, generously extended to them in error.

Both kinds of sufferers—the strong (?), silent ones and
the vociferous complainers—come to Al-Anon in equal
need of help.

I was the silent type. I buried my head deeper in the
sand than an ostrich. I fooled only myself. I'd had several
years of fine AA meetings which, if misery-loving-company
is an answer, had failed me completely. I had learned that
many others faced the same situation but it hadn't done
me much good.

Then came Al-Anon. I was slow to learn even in it but I
did immediately feel there were answers for me and it was
up to me to find them. I knew Al-Anon was meant for me
and for my problems, just as AA was meant for the alcoholic. That was the first great surge toward freedom.

I remember the first time, years and years ago, that I put

Al-Anon to work and risked a slight breach in my hitherto impenetrable wall. We had recently moved. A dearly loved neighbor, just widowed, phoned to say she was going abroad. She was to be in town that afternoon only and would like to come to say goodbye. Naturally I asked her to tea and prepared an impressive one.

Then at noon the blow fell. My husband came home unexpectedly, the worse for wear. He'd seemed all right at breakfast—and I was frantic. Our apartment was about the size of two card-tables; the walls were tissue thin and I could think of no way to reach Dorothy to stop her coming, which was my first impulse. The lovely sandwiches, fancy petits fours, jumbo salted nuts, all mocked me during the ages I waited for her ring.

Then, like the Marines in the movies, as I watched her come up the stairs, Al-Anon came to my rescue. I'd attended only a few meetings but I had learned courage to face the situation.

As she moved toward the bedroom with her hat and coat, I said lightly, "Better bring them here. The body is lying in state in there and he's best not disturbed."

"I'm sorry," she said. "Why didn't you tell me he's sick and I wouldn't have bothered you." "I'm not bothered," I said. "He reunioned with his old outfit last night and celebrated too well. He's just got a hangover—he earned it. I stayed home alone and I'm feeling fine." And I was, suddenly.

She just laughed and said what an unsympathetic, hardboiled Hannah I was and went on to tell how she'd once overindulged and how she suffered. I completely relaxed. No moan or groan from the bedroom upset either of us.

Long before, I thought I had accepted alcoholism as an illness but I very evidently had never accepted the compulsion of it. I'd given it lip-service only.

Newcomers ask why alcoholics drink when they really don't want to, when they know how one drink will inevitably lead to trouble, when they know all the answers and actually long for sobriety. That question still bothers me a little. I now know it is because of compulsion; that they have not yet substituted an equal compulsion against drinking. But since I have whole-heartedly accepted my powerlessness over alcohol, I have further accepted the fact that following the AA program is the alcoholic's business, not mine, and that is the answer I make to newcomers.

I can identify with these troubled newcomers because I once agonized over the same difficulties. They identify with me because they recognize their mistakes when I tell them mine.

Al-Anon is like speaking a language. Even though handling alcoholic problems is not native to our previous experience, through the program we have learned how to meet situations, just as we learn fluency in a foreign tongue.

Al-Anon members have a common bond of experience which brings understanding and enables us to offer help, hope and restored joy in living to those who come to us in despair. We not only speak their language, we have made ourselves bilingual in the alcoholic and non-alcoholic worlds. We should keep fluent.

Thank God for Al-Anon.

Al-Anon's Program Comes to the Rescue

Sometimes my mind does such queer things I begin to question if I really have one. After all the years of Al-Anon, you'd think there'd be no possibility of a negative thought finding houseroom in it, even momentarily.

Such thoughts nevertheless do creep in. Just a month or so ago I shocked myself. True, we had a winter and spring which shouldn't have happened to a dog.

Jack and I had played pat-ball with flu germs so that one or the other was always either coming down with a new go at it or just recuperating from one. Then I followed with a most annoying ear infection, better forgotten now. Just as we began to relax and felt half-human again, our daughter became gravely ill and was hospitalized nearly three months.

Anyhow, the day I shocked myself I was reading the Psalms. Attentively—I thought. But I came upon, "For I alone am afflicted." Further on, something kept nagging at me. I stopped reading, thought a minute and said to myself, "Something's wrong. These are Psalms I'm reading—David, not Job." So I turned back the pages and re-read, correctly this time, "For I am alone and afflicted."

That may not seem as startling to you as it did to me. But to me, "I alone" is the quintessence of self-pity. To some, "Alone and afflicted" may seem to lean a bit to the self-pitying side but not to me. It's just a factual, dispassionate summing-up.

I was amazed and upset that I had subconsciously switched the words around because I hadn't realized I had allowed myself to sink so low. When things were at their worst, in years past, I never indulged in that "poor little me" attitude I always found disgusting. To begin with, I'm not little. Neither have I ever felt that I have been unduly put upon—in fact I have always felt I probably have been blessed beyond my deserts.

But there it was: "I alone," as if I'd been singled out from all others for affliction! That ended the Psalms for that day. I don't know whether I spent the next half hour on the Tenth or the Eleventh Step—I believe it was a combination of both.

I mentally reviewed the past winter and spring in detail. I decided I was physically at a low ebb from illness, that I was not seeing things in proper perspective. I was rebelling at my daughter's illness instead of concentrating on thanking God she was recovering.

The various parts of the program fell into place: I could see where and how I had gone wrong. I had been placing my own will above that of God and, powerless over carrying out either mine or His, I had landed in a mess.

But a wonderful part of Al-Anon's philosophy is that there is always something to be done if you are willing to work at it. Once I realized I had slipped into the trap of self-pity, I could pull up my socks and stop it immediately. I had only to look about me to see how really fortunate I was. I could stop regretting what had happened and begin to be grateful it hadn't been worse.

I could stop putting my will above God's and begin again, more wholeheartedly, to pray for the power to carry out His. I could work harder at "practicing these principles in all my affairs."

People sometimes just coast along, riding on momentum. I believe that's what I had been doing. Not from smugness, I hope; probably more a case of just taking Al-Anon for granted. It took the simple fact of mixing up the order of a few words to shake me out of that complacency. I'm glad I mixed them up. Straightening them out helped straighten me out.

We in Al-Anon Have Priceless Gifts to Give

To MANY PEOPLE, Christmas is a day of giving and of sharing, a heart-warming day of childhood recollections, remembrance of old friends and new, of loving thoughts and wishes for everyone the world over.

We in the Al-Anon Family Group fellowship are among the most fortunate of Earth's creatures because our giving is spread throughout the entire year when we practice our program in all our daily affairs. And we always have priceless gifts to give: restored hope, renewed faith and unselfish love.

Occasionally human frailty traps us into wondering if we really can help others when we have made so many mistakes ourselves. Here Longfellow may give you the lift he did me. Not long ago I happened upon a couple of lines where he said, "Give what you have. To some one, it may be better than you dare to think."

I was preparing a talk to give at a large, very important meeting of Al-Anons and AAs. I wanted to do an outstanding job, worthy of their confidence in inviting me. The theme of the entire day was Recovery Through Knowledge and mine was to be a personal recovery story to close the program.

Naturally I began with the "How sick I was" part—the state from which I recovered through Al-Anon's program. As I jotted down the mistaken things I had done, one sillier than another, some amusing, some tragically burdensome to me, all of them misguided and hurtful, the thought crossed my mind as it has so many times before, "These things you did were so stupid, you fought the First Step so long and so stubbornly, perhaps they'll think you are not worth listening to, that anyone so far off base couldn't recover."

But what could I do? I had done those things and couldn't deny it. They were all I had to tell to point up what I like to think is the recovery I have made. As the song goes, "I've come a long way, Baby!" And I believe I really have helped some people over the years.

It was as I was reviewing my failures that I remembered Longfellow's "It may be better than you dare to think."

Thus I was able to ignore my regret for such a silly, stupid story as mine before the Al-Anon program really changed my life. I concentrated on what had given me the courage and knowledge to overcome my stubborn persistence in errors.

And so I gave my talk. Longfellow was right. I gave what I had and it was better than I had dared to hope, if those who thanked me afterwards weren't just being kind. They said I had shown them mistakes they still were making and had pointed the way to recovery.

The very fact that I had continued so long and so obstinately to mismanage my life, that I had allowed myself to become an utter recluse and yet now could talk to four hundred or more people, gave them hope. They knew that if I could do it, they could. Through Al-Anon, they can.

All of which brings me back to what we of Al-Anon have to give and to share. We can celebrate Christmas every day. We may not have wealth nor material gifts to shower upon others. But we do have the wisdom gained from dearly-bought experience with which to encourage others.

Every day and every person seeking Al-Anon's teachings, is our opportunity to make Christmas last throughout the year. Our gift to all who come to us for help in living with an alcoholic problem is a gift above rubies. In making it we become part of an Al-Anon chain which links the world.

And so, as always, my wish for you is that every holiday joy be yours and may Al-Anon strengthen and guide you all through the year.

Putting the Past to Work for Others

ONE TWO-EDGED facet of life today is the incredible speed of communication. News, good and bad, flashes around the world instantly. Seemingly, at times, most of it is grim.

If we allow ourselves to dwell exclusively upon bad news, we are headed for trouble. That would be like casting up a balance sheet where we counted only the slow-selling merchandise remaining on the shelves, without taking credit for what had been sold profitably.

Perhaps there is little or nothing we can do about some of the events which make us unhappy. But to offset those, we can always remember there is one field in which we are well-experienced, where we can do much to make life happier and easier—for others.

We can now look back upon times when we rebelled at what we then considered an extravagant waste of time and talent. We thought that waste was caused by wanton self-indulgence on the part of our loved one. What turned the screw most tightly, what we found most unforgivable, was that the drinker did not even enjoy the drinking.

That was how many of us were before we embraced the Al-Anon philosophy. But we can see now that every unhappy incident was only a step in the training we needed to mature. Once we learned that alcoholism is an illness, not a positive proof of rejection of our love and concern, we were able to move out of the high and mighty judgment seats in which we had coldly installed ourselves.

We could accept that past experience, not as something visited upon us to bedevil us, but as something to make us grow. Through the success we achieved in applying Al-Anon's program, we were able to stretch out life-saving hands to others still rebelling.

And from the first successful Twelfth Step job we accomplished, we saw our former life in different perspective. It ceased to be an unhappy waste and we came to recognize it as a time of preparation. Without it we would be ill-prepared to help newcomers. We'd be as misguided as the doctor to whom I went for help many years ago. He advised, in well-meant ignorance, that my husband take two drinks every night before dinner. He believed such a practice would solve the problem.

Two things we should do to help others: we should care and we should share. If we accepted all of Al-Anon's blessings as our right, and stopped there, we didn't make the program our own. So long as we know of one person in need of our help, we should not be content to stand idly by.

We have vast experience behind us. Some of it may be exactly what another needs. Al-Anon's teachings showed us how to transmute personal tragedy into strengths which enable us to guide others to the same success. We moved from unhappy darkness into the cheering light of full day with Al-Anon's aid. We ended futile rebellion at every exasperating trifle. We gathered courage and a will to live in ever-increasing serenity and helpfulness.

This is the first month of a whole new year. Let us strive to put our past to work for others in the best, most helpful way we can, every month of this year. Let's make 1970's Twelfth Step work our best yet. Thus, as we have emerged victors in our fight against the past, that success can lead others to the same triumphant outcome.

Anger can be Friend as well as Foe

LONG BEFORE the Sermon on the Mount promised that "the meek shall inherit the earth," an early Psalm advised: "Cease from anger, and forsake wrath . . . the meek shall inherit the earth; and shall delight themselves in the abundance of peace."

It's nice to know that the meek will be lavishly rewarded some day but I've always felt that meekness isn't always everything. I know for a fact that quite a number of angry men have helped to improve the real estate the meek will inherit.

When enough people got angry enough at the widespread air and water pollution in "America the Beautiful," a movement began to clear it up. When greedy lumber companies threatened huge areas of land by denuding them of trees, angry men enforced programs of scientific harvesting and replanting. Even wildlife benefited. Whooping cranes were nearly extinct until angry men took steps to have them protected. Today their numbers, while still small, have greatly increased so that our children's children may still catch a glimpse of them one day.

Angry men and women have a definite place, and a job to do, even in some Al-Anon groups. They don't necessarily make bad friends in clearing up bad situations which threaten group-unity. They do need, usually, to persevere.

Some groups have been unhappy because a Mr. or a Mrs. Al-Anon felt, and took, too great a part in management; permitted no other voice to be heard, no plans to be carried out but their own. Sometimes concerned members could straighten out such situations. Sometimes a group had to be broken up and re-formed into a new, more democratic one.

Then there have been groups which permitted too much talk of spouses until it really amounted to gossip. Wiser heads among them, angry, appalled, concerned—call it what you will—feared that such perversion of Al-Anon's meetings was dangerous to Al-Anon and AA. They determined to replace such loose talk by confining discussions exclusively to Al-Anon's program. They persisted until Al-Anon meetings became real Al-Anon meetings.

Still other members found groups too complacent, provincial and much too preoccupied with local problems. They were stimulated enough by indignation at such limitation of the Al-Anon program that they quietly, gradually, worked to enlarge the groups' horizons until most of them could appreciate their own place in a larger, wider world.

Anger needn't be loud shouting, uncontrolled tirades at another's fault nor unbridled scene-making. It can be a stimulous to better things, a helpful tool for cleaning up bad situations, an energy-producer when it is properly directed.

I believe there is a place for anger in Al-Anon specifically, as well as in the world at large. Temper tantrums are childish exhibitions which should neither be permitted nor confused with good healthy anger. Righteous anger makes all go out and conquer obstacles to Al-Anon's growth and welfare.

Discussion of the Serenity Prayer—Part I

"GOD GRANT ME THE SERENITY TO ACCEPT THE THINGS I CANNOT CHANGE."

By the time we came to Al-Anon, serenity was something we perhaps once had, a word in the dictionary or an item in the newspaper. It gradually had been lost and replaced with a bitter determination to change that "souse" we lived with into a spouse.

Sometimes we did change things. I did, frequently. By staunch opposition I frequently changed a passing idea of a drink into a solid determination to have ten. By thrusting AA on my husband, I lessened its effectiveness—AA is for AAs and they prefer it straight, not filtered through non-alcoholics, ignorant ones at that.

Then came Al-Anon. We saw serenity in action. The first time I found myself laughing when a newcomer said in horror that "He hides bottles," I knew I was on the right road. My life had been a prolonged game of Hide and Seek, when I'd hunt out the bottles he'd hidden so that I could hide them from him. I wasn't playing for fun. Nor did I have it. I was just grim Nemesis.

When told that alcoholism is the alcoholic's problem and only he can solve it, I had to do serious thinking, to weigh just what success had ever come from my efforts to solve the problem. Honesty compelled the admission I had never helped, just added to the difficulties. When told the problem was his, that mine was the problem of how to accept and live with it, a gleam of light shone.

It was only necessary to look back upon the turmoil and frantic disorder in which I had lived, to know that Al-Anon made sense. I recognized that walking the floor in agony until four-thirty in the morning had only exhausted me, until I was too tired and too disturbed to cope with *any* situation. Letting the phone ring because I was afraid to answer it, only frayed my nerves until I was a wreck. Stealing his money hadn't kept him from getting more and it only maddened him and sickened me.

Certainly changes were due and overdue. Those I had made heretofore hadn't pleased me. Al-Anon showed me a whole new world to conquer—right under my own hair, nice and handy!

Once an intelligent person recognizes the stupidity of persisting in useless, wasteful, actually-harmful behavior, there is hope for improvement. Decent sleep helped to an improved disposition; the answered phone frequently was a wrong number, not the police, hospital or employer. I once again began to be human. Serenity did not come overnight—but neither had I lost it overnight.

Serenity did come, however, and it did teach me to distinguish between the things I could change and those I could not. It showed me where to put my efforts. And it paid off—going in circles is much more exhausting than hewing to a line which gets one forward!

Discussion of the Serenity Prayer—Part II

"THE COURAGE TO CHANGE THE THINGS I CAN"

One of the greatest blessings of Al-Anon, to me, is that it gives direction to our lives. All too often, for too long a time, we had passively accepted whatever came, fighting back against whatever hurt us with nagging complaints and shrewish behavior. Neither approach had been effective—each had added unpleasantness to an already unpleasant situation. We had reacted against the stabs but we did nothing positive about them.

Everybody had lost: nagging the alcoholic had confirmed him in his determination to continue drinking. The scenes we created stirred up the family and kept them stirred. We, ourselves, had deteriorated both physically and morally by our lapse of self-control.

Then came Al-Anon, teaching us that alcoholism was the alcoholic's problem, which we could not solve for him. But we could work on our acceptance of the problem, could work on our own reactions to it and could make ourselves calmer, wiser persons to live with and to direct our homes and families.

From being hagridden by all manner of fears, both big and little, Al-Anon showed us how to regain control. It showed us that almost anything we did was an improvement. Thus encouraged, we could go on. It taught us to begin with something small, like walking out on a maudlin argument instead of remaining to add our share to the dispute and thus aggravate the situation. It taught us not to walk the floor all night but to go to bed so that the next day we were better able to cope.

In a word, Al-Anon gave us hope. And with hope, we had an impulse toward bettering ourselves. We began to see the things we could not change but God gave us courage to begin changing those we could. With success in changing the small things, our courage grew so that we could attack those more important. Our lives began to straighten out. We prayed for courage to change what we could and directed our energies toward that—we stopped drifting and began aiming, and working, toward an orderly, useful life.

Discussion of the Serenity Prayer—Part III

"AND THE WISDOM TO KNOW THE DIFFERENCE."

There is a great comfort in the thought that wisdom can be attained by all manner of persons. One needn't go to a great university to search for it. Inherent in a fortunate few, the rest of us can achieve a reasonable degree of wisdom if we give ourselves a chance.

I remember an old neighbor in Montana who was wise—

yet she could neither read nor write. She taught me a lot. One spring the ranch boys brought Marggy a newly-born pig. The sow had too many to cope with and they thought we'd like to try. Marggy was five and enchanted. But piglets weren't meant for humans to raise. This one quickly died. I was in a quiet dither. Marggy had never seen death and I was at a loss to make her understand, to soften the blow.

Fortunately old Annie was there; she took over. She got Marggy a box, set her to gathering moss and wild flowers and pretty stones for a grave. All the time she talked of a pig-heaven and how lovely the little pig looked. Marggy was left with no scar from that first encounter with death, thanks to the instinctive wisdom of our unlettered friend.

I have often been grateful to Annie for this and for the other things she unconsciously taught me of ways to handle difficult situations. All too often, it seems to me, we give up too easily. We say we can't do thus and so because we don't know how to go about it. But if we *want* it enough, I believe we can get the needed wisdom through this prayer. We'll never get it by flying off the handle when something displeases us. We'll never get it if we always talk and never think. We'll never get it through the care and feeding of grudges. Nor through fear.

But anybody can build upon the inherent good born in all of us. By thoughtful and prayerful consideration of what troubles us, we can find the wise way out. We can determine what is best for everyone if we forget ourselves: my own fear of Marggy's being hurt by Piglet's death confused me—Annie thought only of Marggy and what would help her.

When we have attained even a modicum of wisdom, that little bit will show us which things we can change, which we can't and should never even try to alter.

But for the Grace of God

THIS SLOGAN, I BELIEVE, is used more by AAs than by Al-Anons. An AA friend told me she used it on every Twelfth Step call she ever made. No matter in what stage she found the person, "But for the Grace of God" still was useful: if the woman was close to DTs, Nancy thanked God for her own sobriety which had brought her past that danger point; if the woman was resentful, Nancy thanked God for the serenity which had helped her overcome her own resentments, from which, but for the Grace of God, she might still be suffering.

When this slogan does come up in Al-Anon, it is usually brought to our attention by someone who is acute enough, and detached enough to recognize how accidental this whole business of alcoholism is. Any one of us might have been the alcoholic, but for the Grace of God, since alcoholism is an illness. In my rebellion against compulsive drinking I used to protest, swear it would have been better had I been the alcoholic in our family. Long ago, Al-Anon taught me what I should have known before, that God knows better than I.

As a non-alcoholic, I have been spared the unbearable remorse, the killing sense of guilt, the self-loathing that alcoholics suffer until they make peace with themselves in AA. But for the Grace of God, the lightning could have struck me, rather than my husband.

Thus, if any trace of smugness remains in any of us when we see some wretched creature struggling with his affliction, let's pause a moment and remember, "But for the Grace of God, there go I." From the uproar we managed to create just living with the problem, let's contemplate the hell we'd have raised with the problem itself. I'm

sure God knew his business when he made me the Al-
Anon, not the alcoholic. I thank Him and I hope I never
forget to be grateful.

Al-Anon's "Three Important Days"

LIKE GAUL, DIVIDED in three parts, Time is divided into
the past, the present and the future—Yesterday, Today and
Tomorrow.

In Al-Anon you frequently hear that Yesterday is gone
and nothing can be done about it. That's almost true—you
can't change what actually happened. But you certainly
can change your thinking about it. If someone did you an
incomprehensible hurt, instead of nursing a grudge for-
evermore, you can put yourself in the other's place, sort
out what made him do it and, through understanding, heal
that hurt. Yesterday does have a place in showing you how
best to live Today.

Tomorrow is a different matter. It is out of your hands,
except as you too try to prepare to make the best use of it.
You can no more live in the future than you can in the
past. If you've made a mess of Today, you can just hope
there'll be another day when you can do better. You can
determine to do better and work on that.

Today—this very moment—is all you are sure of. And
that flashing instant has gone to join the past even before
you are aware of it. With this dizzy spin of Time the only
safe way to make each moment count is to make our Al-
Anon program so much an integral part of you that right
responses are habitual—you can't go wrong following Al-
Anon's teaching. With them, there's no regret for Yesterday. There's guidance for Today and hope for Tomorrow.

The Lord's Prayer

IT'S A GOOD THING Al-Anon and AA don't have to choose
between the two prayers most closely associated with
them—the Lord's Prayer and the Serenity Prayer. Each
contains fundamentals of the program.

Just as we close each meeting with the Lord's Prayer, it
seems very appropriate that we close the FORUM year
with a consideration of how it fits into our program. AA
took its program in bits and pieces from here, there and
almost everywhere. Al-Anon, in turn, took its program
from AA, unashamedly borrowing, adapting where necessary which was not often, and went forward from there.

The unity of Al-Anon is well expressed where we all
acknowledge a common Father. The concept of His power
is indicated when we place Him in heaven, well above our
mortal effort. Our goal of being restored to sanity is in the
words "Thy kingdom come" because the mess we once
made of our lives was surely not to His liking.

We express the Third Step in almost the same words
when we say "Thy will be done on earth as it is in
Heaven." And asking for our daily bread—not food for a
whole lifetime, not for next year nor next month, but for
our daily bread—couldn't be closer to the 24 hour program. Then we can hardly ask forgiveness for trespasses we
don't acknowledge as wrongs, so the moral inventory is
implied there.

Finally, the Eleventh Step is certainly close to our peti-
tion that we not be led into temptation but delivered from
evil, because we know His will for us could not be that of
continued wrongdoing.

In one way or another, a tremendous part of our program is contained in the Lord's Prayer. One can hear and

feel a special plea when it is said together in meetings. Any prayer is a good prayer but this one, peculiarly adapted to our needs, is our best one.

Listen and Learn!

DURING THE YEAR we plan to discuss what might be called valiant adjuncts to our basic guides, the Steps and Traditions. We'll discuss not only the slogans but what may well become slogans some time.

Since this is the beginning of a new year it seems appropriate to begin with a new precept: LISTEN AND LEARN! Whether we were driven to Al-Anon or came along willingly, we did come and we learned, so we can take the second part for granted. But some of us have difficulty with the first: LISTEN. We can learn faster if we listen properly.

Some time ago a woman came to our group so resentful of her son's behavior that she could speak of nothing else: she had done everything for him—paid his debts, bought his clothes, given him money (he was in his mid-forties) and put up with his uncontrolled drinking. And now, in payment for all her love and care, he'd taken up with *"Some Woman!"*

We thought her visit was her first exposure to Al-Anon; to our amazement we learned she'd attended many meetings years ago. Although she said she came for help—it was evident she needed it badly—she never stopped talking long enough to listen to any suggestion.

Every member of the group tried to help her. She talked everyone down and left the meeting a bit more confirmed in her conviction that she was a helpless victim of unmitigated selfishness. Had she listened, even a moment, windows of hope would have been opened to her; she'd have learned how best to cope with her own problems and even, perhaps, to allow her son to cope with his.

At first it is difficult to listen with an open mind; we don't realize how closed our minds are on certain subjects—especially those which have hurt us. But any kind of listening is better than continual talking. Some day, if we listen instead of talk, something someone says gets through to us and our prejudices. We then begin the long and rewarding process of learning to live with serenity and confidence.

Easy Does It

CONSIDERING THIS easy-to-believe, but hard-to-practice slogan, it would be inappropriate to hammer away at it, as all of us sometimes feel like doing in handling various Al-Anon problems.

Dealing with a new member's closed mind, for instance, can drive you frantic—you scurry around in every corner of your mind to find words that will reach that person—whereas, if you just took it easy, bided your time, someone else in your group might do an even better job.

Here, then, are thoughts of what Easy Does It (or take it easy) means to me. It means not gulping down all Twelve Steps in one undigestible lump. Some can be taken easier than others, and not necessarily in numerical order. You needn't get in a swivet if you have difficulty with the First Step—many of us do. Keep working on it. When you regress from it, recognize the fact instantly and guard against further regression. Don't brand yourself a complete failure.

If you think all your shortcomings are due to living with

an alcoholic, arrested or practicing, give consideration to taking an inventory. If the thought of taking one upsets you, wait a little. You'll do a better job on it when you know even more of the program. And be sure to do it on a day when your halo isn't hurting your head.

There's nothing brand new about the principles of the Al-Anon program. They've been around a long time; have worn well, so it isn't necessary for you to improve them; just try to live by them daily.

Easy Does It doesn't mean sitting on the small of the back with heels above the head as in the comic strips. Rather, to me at least, it means a considered appraisal of a calm, unblustering approach to daily problems; an approach that will not add fuel to a blaze but will so dampen it down as to prevent a new conflagration.

Alcoholics are volatile people to live with, and their non-alcoholic spouses are not necessarily phlegmatic. All of us can use Easy Does It. It is a reliable guidepost and all of us can benefit hugely from it.

Let Go and Let God

To ANYONE who had no difficulty with the First Step, practicing this slogan will, I believe, come easily. But if that "powerless over alcohol" bit was as difficult for you to accept as it was for me, I think you may have the same struggle with letting go.

To begin with, this slogan does not mean "Let Go and Let George Do It." Not at all. It says let God and it means God, your Higher Power, Fate, or whatever belief you live by. It means that you take a back seat and accept whatever answer is given your prayer, your request or your best efforts to keep your hands off another's life.

I never took over our family finances; I did not interfere with the relationship between my husband and my daughter; I never acted as the head of the family. My whole time was spent in trying to circumvent that first drink. I constantly besieged God with advice on how to keep my husband from it, and I supplemented this advice with practical "help" on carrying it out—like running him past a bar so he wouldn't stop off for a quickie.

I never realized the incongruity of such witless behavior. It was only when I really accepted the fact that *I* was powerless over alcohol that I could see what "Let Go and Let God" really meant: to me they are both parts of the same whole, and both have shown me just where I come in.

My husband's problem is separate and distinct from mine. I have to keep my hands off and allow him to solve it. God is infinitely wiser than I. I have seen the mess which I formerly made of our situation and which I continued to make until I learned what the First Step and Let Go and Let God was all about. I continued to make that mess in spite of all the evidence I saw in Al-Anon that the Higher Power's hands were better on the reins than mine.

When I did let go and let God, I didn't give up anything which belonged to me—I relinquished something I should never have taken over. I returned it to the proper hands and two of us benefited.

Think

AMONG THE MANY fortunate influences to which I was exposed in school, was that of Dean Flint. She was a full professor of English, a widow, and mother of two sons. Part of the creed she lived by, and you can see what a lasting impression it made on me, was that it is the business of every parent to see that the succeeding generation is better than his own.

My daughter and I have never seen eye-to-eye on this: she says human nature can't be changed. I say it has changed, and for the better. We no longer put a starving man into prison for snatching a loaf of bread; we don't kill or cripple seven and eight year old children for life by letting them work fourteen hours a day in unheated attics or basements; we no longer visit mental hospitals, seeking to be entertained by the antics of inmates. We *have* progressed. We also now recognize alcoholism as a disease, not a disgrace.

Some people still say you cannot teach old dogs new tricks. But it is my belief that man is not a dog. Not only does he have two less legs, he has an ability to think. And it is in this ability to think that he can look for help in making each succeeding generation at least a little bit better than the preceding one.

No thinking man can buy a new overcoat and hang it up beside two others, still warm and serviceable, without thinking another man is walking cold streets, shivering and uncomfortable. When he thinks of this, he gives the two away to Good Will or the Salvation Army. No thinking woman, during a milk strike, with a freezer full of food and feeding adults only, can snatch the last carton of milk from a woman with a small child.

Think! Imagine where you could be if you forgot everything as soon as it happened; if you acted always upon impulse, without considering anyone else; if you always rode off in all directions from any and all situations.

A few moments' thought can lead you to the solution of some problems; others may take hours or days. But by taking thought, sometimes by asking help of others, the proper solution can be found. And the whole world may be better off. Certainly for those living with an alcoholic, Al-Anon's thinking is priceless.

First Things First

WHAT BROUGHT YOU to Al-Anon? Help for yourself or for someone dear to you? It really doesn't matter because you soon learned that the most important thing in your life was to regain control of yourself. Living with a problem too big for you to solve alone had made inroads on your health, spirit and courage.

This, then, was the beginning. If you listened at meetings with an open mind, you learned that you needed help in regaining these qualities. You saw that others had attained all three, through following the Al-Anon program.

Especially in the beginning, this slogan "First Things First" is vitally important. If it is kept constantly in mind you will always be aware of your goals: acceptance and serenity. It will help you always to sift the important things from the unimportant; it will show you what should be done today and what can wait for tomorrow; and it will re-establish order in your life.

From spinning in a dizzying whirl over every mishap, it will show you just where to put your efforts; after all, a paper cut needs less attention than a severed artery, and "First Things First" shows you which is which, if you stop quietly to evaluate them. Gradually, with this recognition of degrees of importance, you stop that old spinning around; you gain detachment and you see where you need to put your effort.

If you came to Al-Anon for help for yourself, constant practice of determining which things come first has helped you. If you even came for help for a dear one, you may have gained it also with the calmer, more stable atmosphere you have established around you. That by-product does not always result, but you are infinitely better able to cope, once you begin to live by recognizing that certain things must and should come first, and which they are.

Words to Live By

THREE WORDS deserve to stand among our slogans: "Why Not Try?" Early in our Al-Anon days, and for many of us long before Al-Anon, when things got bad we simply gave up, went to pieces in one way or another. Thus we contributed handsomely to our own downfall. It took various parts of the program, the example of the group, and a new lease on life to prod us into attempting to overcome our indifference, our lethargy, our rejection of the world.

When I remember a much older friend of my older sister, a woman then in her middle or late sixties, it always makes me think of those who simply give up, who never consider anything but the status quo, and take it as permanent.

One icy, stormy day when Abby should never have gone out, she slipped and broke her hip in a most peculiar and dangerous way. Her doctor did all that was possible but was afraid she would never walk again. Abby asked for training in strengthening exercises and worked at them so that in three months she walked without a limp!

Then, exactly a year later, she fell again, again breaking the same hip in the same horrible way. This time the doctor was convinced she'd surely spend the rest of her life in a wheelchair. But Abby would have none of it. Again she set herself to the special exercises and again she walked. The doctor called it a miracle and it was: a miracle of determination.

Nothing but that determination to overcome a handicap helped Abby to overcome a physical catastrophe. Had she sat back and accepted the handicap, she'd still be in a wheelchair. But she determined to exhaust every possibility of help before giving up and kept trying.

There is something to help most of us in our difficulties. There is no reason for us to continue to accept them supinely. We can improve our plight, even if we cannot eliminate the cause of our distress. Why not try? We have nothing to lose and everything to gain.

Keep an Open Mind

MOST OF US have seen crabbed, soured, middle-aged or really old people, who have let life overcome them. Very often they have slitted eyes, pinched noses and straight-line mouths—gashes instead of lips. Naturally they are not attractive, receptive-looking persons. It is as difficult to get a new idea into their minds as it is to fire them with enthusiasm for the frug or the watusi.

Age is not necessarily a prerequisite to a permanently closed mind. Unfortunately, disappointment and unhappiness can lead many young persons to shut out new ideas and experiences, perhaps because some unlucky chance had thrown them back upon themselves, made them distrustful of almost everything.

To rule out all new ideas because a few proved unhelpful, or distasteful, would be as stupid as to stop eating because one had bitten into an apple, rotten at the core.

Many people come to Al-Anon in bitterness and frustration; some of the things they first hear seem incredible and unrealistic: the idea that the most fruitful place to begin work is upon one's own self is unwelcome, especially if "that old so-and-so" still drinks.

The main thing for established members, as well as newcomers, as I see it, is to give one's self every chance for mental and spiritual growth by weighing all new approaches or ideas. If we automatically rule out each offer of help, each new conception presented to us, block out each new experience, we limit ourselves to a very restricted field in which we have few opportunities to enlarge our horizons.

Each automatic rejection of a new idea makes it easier to reject the next; the habit of refusal fastens itself tight upon us. Not every new idea is right for us but we should give each due consideration.

Keeping an open mind is our way of ensuring easy accessibility to the greatest amount of help and happiness possible.

Live and Let Live

THIS SLOGAN is double-barreled. It would be well for each of us to keep both parts constantly in mind. Naturally, the first part pertains to us, personally; the second part admonishes us to allow others to live their lives.

That first "Live" should prod us into a consideration of our own lives. Are we letting never-to-return days slip by us in discontented, unhappy, aimless repudiation of what we could really accomplish if we but had the will to stir ourselves? Grant that things are about as bad as could be: our partner is still drinking; our children are getting out of hand; we are in debt; we have few friends left and we avoid them and our families as much as possible. We live practically alone, with fear and dread.

Except that my daughter never got out of hand, all those things were once true of me. And I couldn't have cared less. Sullen and sick at heart as I then was, I had so accustomed myself to indifference to the world about me that almost nothing penetrated the gloom I drew about myself.

John Donne said, "No man is an island." But I had islanded myself. It took Al-Anon, plus close association with truly wonderful Al-Anoners like Lois, Anne, Sue and Dot to stimulate me to attempt a bridge back to a more normal outlook. My early work at what we called our Clearing House further fired me with courage to return to a living life, instead of persisting in a living death. No one can really live without a compelling interest; Al-Anon became that—the focus of my new life. Thus, though tardily, I put the first "Live" into action.

The first thing to be done, if you have given up as I had, is to find some interest which will keep you from that spineless indifference to everything about you. You may be fortunate in having some talent which will give added stimulus to your Al-Anon work.

Then, just as you must have a real life for yourself, you should, in gratitude and fairness, be willing to allow others to have their lives, their opinions and their say. We all know the danger of allowing one person, no matter how wise and experienced, to dominate our groups. Not only does this prevent a free exchange of ideas, but it also prevents the spiritual growth of other members.

Sometimes it is necessary for one to learn by making a mistake. Truly wise and experienced "older members" will make every effort to allow newcomers to mature healthfully in this program by letting them live the program at their own pace; they offer what wisdom they have but don't insist on it.

Most of us would do well to keep "Live and Let Live" in the forefront of our minds, no matter how long we have been in Al-Anon.

Who Said "This Is a Selfish Program"?

FEW THINGS in our program are as confusing, to my mind, as this statement. Many people give it various interpretations. Generally speaking, I believe there must be a better word for what is meant than "selfish."

The worst interpretation I ever heard came from a woman who accepted it enthusiastically at its face value: right out in meeting she said, unblushingly, "I certainly agree this is a selfish program. If my husband dies from alcoholism, I'll have his life insurance. If he gets the AA program, he'll sober up and be able to support me. Either way, I'll be taken care of."

Selfish, according to Webster, means "Caring unduly or supremely for one's self; regarding one's own comfort, advantage, etc., in disregard or at the expense of others . . ."

Certainly no one who has really tried to live the Twelve Steps, especially in making an honest effort to "carry the message to others and to practice these principles in all our affairs," can be doing so in disregard or at the expense of others.

I believe "selfish" in this case means that the program is a *personal* one: no one can practice it for us—we must make the effort ourselves. We must look within ourselves to determine where we went wrong, and stir ourselves to make things right. We ourselves have to put the principles into practice.

Granted that we are heartily sick and tired of the mess we have made of living with an alcoholic, we may *enter* the program from the selfish motive of attaining peace within ourselves. But from the moment we actually begin to practice the Al-Anon program, I believe "selfish" changes to "personal" and we work it, not only for ourselves but for anyone else in need of help.

Discussion of "We Have No Dues or Fees"

AL-ANON is a membership organization. That is to say, members share in and determine its decisions and responsibilities. Groups, from the beginning, were polled on all matters affecting Al-Anon as a whole. Today we have delegates to the World Service Conference who accept this responsibility for their states and provinces. Groups are autonomous but concern themselves, generally, with the common good of Al-Anon rather than with their own rights and privileges.

Groups have little need of money: enough for rent, refreshments if served, and literature. Because large amounts in treasuries may cause problems, Al-Anon has never laid stress on big collections and by policy refuses contributions from outside sources.

As in AA, the secretary's usual announcement when passing the basket is, "We have no dues or fees but we do have expenses." Such a practice is fine as far as groups are concerned.

Our World Service Office, however, is a different case. It has great need of money and can look only to Al-Anon members to supply it. In little more than 15 years Al-Anon has grown from a few groups in the U.S. and Canada, to a worldwide network of some 3,600 groups. (Note: Now over 5,000)

In the 2nd quarter of 1967 alone, an average of 69 groups a month were formed and 86 proposed groups a month wrote for assistance. Nearly 25,000 FORUMS were mailed in those 3 months (over 10,000 free to groups), free Directories were sent each group; 1,386 copies of letters offering Al-Anon help were sent to institutional and prison groups. Postage alone has averaged over $900 a month all this year. (Now over $1,400 a month.)

Substantial sums, such as these figures indicate, are a bit frightening when one considers the tenuous nature of our finances, which depends primarily upon voluntary contributions of members. It frequently seems to me that we should add a bit to that oft-heard announcement: "We have no dues or fees but we do have gratitude!"

Not only do we have gratitude for what Al-Anon has done for us, we have a firm determination that it will continue to exist so that all who are yet to come may find the same help.

We cannot, in conscience, handicap our World Services Office by lack of support. That support must come from the members, far and wide, so that Al-Anon's work may not only continue as at present but expand as needed.

Discussion of the First Step

"We admitted we were powerless over alcohol—that our lives had become unmanageable."

A still-popular cliché is "One must learn to walk before he can run." No one who ever watched a baby's first steps needs to be told this twice.

A few walk easily. Most put blood, sweat, toil and tears into the effort. Frustration irks them endlessly.

The more I think of Al-Anon's First Step, the more I see that it is like a baby's. It has to be taken—no progress can be made without it. But for most Al-Anons it is the most difficult.

A very few are blessed with accepting it immediately. They grasp it at once and never let go. My own daughter understood it years before I did. She was 13 when I learned and told her alcoholism was a compulsive disease which the victim could not control, once he had a drink.

Shortly thereafter things got difficult. Her father spoke sharply to her for almost the first time in her life. Afraid she'd be hurt, when we were alone I explained he'd misunderstood her or he'd never have spoken as he did.

"Don't worry," she said, matter of factly. "He'd been drinking." "What difference does that make?" I asked.

"When he's drinking he's not my father and I don't bother at all." Appalled, I said, "Drink or no drink, he is *still your father.*"

"Oh no. When he's not drinking, *he is himself and then he's my father.*"

It took me years, literally, to see she was exactly right. When an alcoholic drinks, alcohol is in control, not the alcoholic, not the person at all.

Even at that early age, my daughter saw that she herself was powerless over alcohol and that her father was too.

With this instinctive understanding of the problem, no harm ever was done to their relationship and no father and daughter ever could be closer.

Few wives or husbands attain this complete understanding easily. The drinker seems to make sense a lot of the time, though he may be talking in a blackout.

With the burden of guilt which haunts them all, the

alcoholic, when drinking, lashes out verbally at his partner, trying to equalize the responsibility.

One definition of sober is "not affected by passion or prejudice." According to this, few partners are truly sober when the other is drinking and raving.

Thus the "sober" spouse lashes back. Feelings are hurt. Misunderstandings, often serious ones, arise; harm is done. True acceptance of the fact that one is powerless over alcohol would save both heartaches and headaches.

You, as well as your partner, are powerless over alcohol. The quicker you stop trying to be an irresistible force meeting an immovable object, the quicker you will gain serenity.

The time spent concentrating your energies on trying to control another's habits and life, is that much time spent in prolonging an unmanageable situation—it's time wasted.

You are powerless over alcohol; your life, pre–Al-Anon, became unmanageable, if you're like most of us. But you're NOT powerless over yourself. Al-Anon, if you'll allow it to help you, will show you how to control yourself, to straighten out your own life.

Once you recognize alcoholism as a disease, over which both you and your partner are powerless, you have a firm base on which to build.

You do not have the disease and cannot cure it. But you do bear scars from living in turmoil. Had you understood the nature of the disease in the beginning, those scars would have been avoided.

You do, however, now have Al-Anon. You can remake your life, and yourself, if you stop this losing battle and concentrate on a way of life which will help you, your family and the alcoholic also. A tranquil home life offers everyone an inducement to do better.

There's one pre-eminent caution about this Step. Never think of it as a "once and for all time" job.

We are all too human. We all like things done our way. We must keep in mind our own limitations and our own expectations. We must allow the other person to have his.

Discussion of the Second Step

"Came to believe that a Power greater than ourselves could restore us to sanity."

People who have lived years with a practicing alcoholic mate, usually have little difficulty in acknowledging that their lives have become unmanageable. Until they understand the First Step fully, and really take it, they feel a great burden of responsibility.

They feel they have failed to understand the alcoholic; have done or not done things to help him keep sober; their love is in some way lacking or it would have prevented the excess.

Thus, and it is very understandable when they are living in such confusion, they live with a constant burden of guilt on their shoulders, a sense of having been tried and found wanting.

They have relied upon themselves too long, have tried to be supermen when they were merely mortal.

To all these weary, hopeless, desperate people, this Second Step comes as a gift straight from the blue. Many of them once had some belief, some religion, but had long since separated from it in protest. Now, after fully accepting the First Step, they are able to see what reliance upon themselves alone had done to them.

They are ready to give up their morbid sense of responsibility, are able to see that, of themselves, they can go nowhere but further down.

Into their despair comes a realization that *something*

can help them: something bigger than themselves—some call it God, some their Higher Power, some the Group Spirit and some any number of other things.

Whatever they call it, it brings release to them. By themselves, they got into a mess; this Higher Power can help them straighten it out if they cooperate.

Many have lived so long in the ruinous alcoholic atmosphere that their personalities have changed; they have deviated far from normal behavior. The changes in many cases were so gradual, or so long-established that at first it was difficult to recognize them as abnormal.

With a recognition of and dependence upon the Higher Power, however, they begin to see how far they have deteriorated. With trust in the Higher Power they set themselves to return to normality.

This Step, like so many of the others, is at once a great comfort and a greater challenge. It really separates the men from the boys to root out that stubborn resistance to the Higher Power and to cooperate with it fully.

In years of Al-Anon and AA talks, I have never heard anyone tell of calling upon God or his Higher Power in vain. Many tell of difficulty with the "spiritual angle" but come to accept and rely on it. And it works.

A Discussion of the Third Step

"Made a decision to turn our will and our lives over to the care of God as we understood Him."

In Al-Anon, as in AA, there are no musts; the program is not religious. It is open to all. It is, however, a spiritual one and for those who believe in God this Step logically follows the first two.

Once you have acknowledged your inability to cope with things beyond your control and discovered that your own ineptness has geometrically increased your problems, you become willing to look elsewhere for help.

Those who believe in God, I have observed, seem to have an easier time accepting help. But it is not necessary to believe in Him—we have successful agnostics and atheists in Al-Anon; it just seems to take them a bit longer to get the program.

Some turn to God for help. Others call on a Higher Power, which can be anything from the group spirit to something outside of and bigger than the person himself.

I said the fortunate ones turn to God because it has always seemed to me that these people have a quiet sureness about them, an ease of acceptance, that the others slightly lack. Very possibly I am wrong. Each of us accepts all we personally can and it seems sufficient.

We come to Al-Anon with demonstrated failure behind us, with a shaken reliance upon our own judgment and management. We are looking for a way out—a way up.

Many despairing persons once had a firm belief and established communication with God. But through years of desperate loneliness, vain hope, unhappiness and ever-increasing strain, many gave up all pretense of belief. They went it alone, in a stark, bitterly miserable way.

Al-Anon's first two steps, however, showed them their record of a great deal less than success. Depending only upon themselves led them to the mess which drove them to Al-Anon to seek any way out.

By this time, those who once believed in God were ready to try anything—even going back to God—to lead them out of the morass of the unrewarding lives they were living.

Fortunately for them, it is a loving God they turned to, one who easily overlooked their lapse.

234

At this point they made a decision to turn their lives and their wills over to His care, each according to his understanding.

They intended to keep living up to this decision.

But having indulged themselves so long, they found it a difficult resolution to sustain.

They had spent years running everything as much their own way as they could, had come to look upon themselves as the last word in authority. Shedding such long-established habits cannot be done overnight.

They can, however, concentrate on changing themselves as fast as they are able to digest our program. If they keep an open mind, the group can show them where they go wrong, should they have a relapse.

Slowly for some, miraculously fast for others, order is restored in their lives. Courage returns. Life again becomes worth living.

(Editor's Note: As was said at the beginning, there are no musts in Al-Anon. No one has to accept any or all of the above. It is a personal interpretation, according to my own experience. Should you disagree, you should work out your own interpretation . . . there's plenty of room. It would be interesting to compare any such differences.)

Discussion of the Fourth Step

"Made a searching and fearless moral inventory of ourselves."

Anyone who takes the Al-Anon program seriously knows that conscientious, thoughtful attention must be given to each step. There is no leaping up and down the Twelve, as children do when playing games.

They were carefully planned so that each follows logically upon the preceding one. Thus, having had the courage to admit our powerlessness over alcohol, to recognize that our lives had become unmanageable, we were able to admit that help from a Power greater than ourselves was necessary to us and we became willing to let that Power help us. These first three Steps are the foundation for the fourth.

It is only after we have thoroughly studied, accepted and put the first three into practice that we are, I believe, ready for this Fourth one.

We cannot jump at it while we still believe we are responsible for our partner's excess, while we still are trying to influence or promote abstinence and are living in self-created turbulence. To be successful in this Step, we must have reached a measure of detachment, to have gained an unbiased judgment of ourselves.

This detachment, this unbiased judgment is essential because, to my way of thinking, the most important word in this Step is "fearless."

It is useless, I believe, to take an inventory if we are still wallowing in excuses: "I wouldn't do this if he/she hadn't done that." "I am sober. The mess isn't MY fault!"

It is only when we are completely ready to look conditions straight in the face, to acknowledge our part in worsening an already bad situation, that there's any value in taking it.

This takes courage enough to acknowledge to ourselves that in the past we frequently added fresh fuel to blazing scenes that were better damped down; we can say to ourselves we did it in ignorance, and with the best intentions. But we have to acknoweldge the harm we did, so that we won't continue doing it.

We also have to have enough objectivity to give ourselves credit for the things we did well. A true balance sheet always has to have two columns: a debit and a credit one.

When we can fearlessly examine our past behavior, judging only our own actions and reactions, then is the time, and not before, to my mind, to take a searching inventory.

Discussion of the Fifth Step

"Admitted to God, to ourselves and to another human being the exact nature of our wrongs."

The inventory Steps, Four through Ten, have a certain inescapable momentum. They also show the deepest possible understanding of human beings.

First is the fearless moral inventory, in which we seek out our weaknesses and strengths. If the inventory is really fearless and exact, it usually points the way to this Fifth Step because we cannot bear to leave things in the mess they are in.

All the Steps are progressive: admitting our wrongs to God is usually easy—most of us feel He knows them already. Admitting them to ourselves is part of the fearless inventory. The catch comes in admitting them to another human being.

I do not believe I am unique in putting the best face possible on the things I do. Unconsciously, if there are two ways to present a situation, I tend to give myself a break in choosing the less revolting one. And right there is the value of "another human being."

It is more difficult to lie to another person than to one's self; if lie is too strong a word, then the impulse to present an exact picture is stronger when another person is involved. The urge to do a wholesale job of recognizing responsibility is strengthened by the effort to make that other person understand. We can do it only by complete honesty and detachment.

Putting things into words, which must be done to make another person understand, is the most potent factor (to me) in this Step. It ensures an exact realization of wrongs done. Furthermore, that other human being has a responsibility: he or she can prevent you from going overboard in an orgy of self-recrimination; he can recognize your hits and misses if the picture you paint is a too-exaggeratedly black one.

It seems to me that one cannot take a true inventory too early in our program. One must have time to learn quite a bit about it or the inventory will not be valid. Newcomers tend to blame themselves for everything they've done, especially when a partner is still drinking. Sometimes everything they've done has been wrong but not always and not usually. They need help in recognizing where they were right—and encouragement to continue. That's where another human being can stretch out a helping hand.

If the time is right for you to take the Fourth Step, don't leave it at that. It's only one part of the next six—all equally necessary. The Fifth Step, rightly taken, lays an invaluable foundation for those to follow.

Discussion of the Sixth Step

"Were entirely ready to have God remove all these defects of character."

Two words of this Step seem to me of paramount importance: "entirely" and "all." This Step depends upon a fearless inventory and an admission to one's self, to God and to another person the exact nature of wrongs.

Granting those, comes the state of mind in which to take this Step; every one of us hates a grudging gift and that old saw, "God loves a cheerful giver," is still around. Thus we must work to ensure that we want most emphatically to be rid of these defects, that we are glad to put them behind us, ALL of them.

"All these defects" frequently reminds me of times I've determined to clean out catchalls: bits and pieces of clutter which have accumulated over the years. The day comes when I determine to toss them out in one fell swoop. But my eyes light on a yellowed letter—my first love letter! Puppy love, yes, but what a thrill it was. I've had it for years and forgotten it. Can I bear now to give it the toss? Can't I keep just this? Then I remember my resolve to put an end to all the accumulation. Out it goes.

Faults, self-indulgences, can be like that ancient letter. We've had them so long we perhaps forget they are there. But if we aim at true spiritual growth, can we give up lying and continue stealing?

Granted these last are an exaggeration, it's only a matter of degree. Can we pick and choose which defects to give up if we honestly take this Step? Thus, all means ALL and we ready ourselves for the next Step where we ask God to remove them.

Discussion of the Seventh Step

"Humbly asked Him to remove our shortcomings."

To achieve success with this Step we cannot approach it with the attitude of one asking a doctor to remove a physical defect, an ugly wart or a troublesome ingrown nail.

True, these are part of us. But they developed by themselves, from a cause unknown to us and beyond our control.

Character defects are a different thing: if we have done proper homework on the Steps preceding this one, we well know—or should—just how such defects began. We probably have spent years in the care and nurture of them; they are now so deeply entrenched in our daily lives they are difficult to uproot.

Most commonly such defects are resentment, self-pity and instant blame of another person. None of these is a desirable response to a given situation. All, in fact, stem from a lack of understanding of ourselves. With Al-Anon's guiding light we can recognize them as shortcomings within ourselves.

With this recognition and with the desire to attain the spiritual growth promised by the Al-Anon program, we can do our best to overcome these and other faults we have picked up over the troubled years.

Perhaps there are perfect human beings in the world. I have not met any in my group nor among my other friends. Depending solely upon ourselves, we run into trouble, are brought up short by failure. Thus we ask for help.

And that help is unfailing if we seek it in the right way. We should not demand it as a right, sitting back, arrogantly telling our Higher Power what to do to make us better people.

First we do our utmost to overcome our faults ourselves. Then, with full appreciation of our own shortcomings and failures, we humbly ask His help. Humility is really a sense of proportion, a yardstick of what we are worth. So it is only after we have done our best, and know it is not good enough, that we can humbly ask for help and know it will be given us.

Discussion of the Eighth Step

"Made a list of all persons we had harmed, and became willing to make amends to them all."

One thing to remember when working on the Steps is that they are not just forward-going Steps: they rely heavily upon what already is past. They are like a nursemaid we had when young who never said "back and forth" as most of us do; she always went "forth and back," which is what we have to do when we begin working on a new Step.

This one is not difficult if we have a thorough-going inventory behind us. Such a review of the past shows who was hurt by our reaction to our own hurt.

A list of those persons, in black and white or graven deep in our minds, is necessary to prepare us to take the next—the Ninth Step. We have to see what wrongs we did and whether they hurt another, before we can work on becoming willing to make amends.

Frequently the greatest harm we did was to ourselves, by loss of control. We became unhappy, impatient and struck out at anyone near us because we were ourselves upset. Sometimes the other person understood and refused to be harmed by such injustice. In this case we damaged only ourselves by uncontrolled behavior.

Once we understand the damage done to ourselves, the best amends we can make is to forgive ourselves and to forget all of it, except just enough to prevent us from ever succumbing again.

Other persons, however, did not always understand what made us act as we did. Children, especially, most frequently were victims of our frustrations. They often suffered in an unhappy world of their own.

Many parents simply are unable or unwilling to admit they hurt their own children—regardless of cause. I believe this is frequently why some Al-Anon parents shy away from encouraging their children to go to Alateen. Consciously or unconsciously, they feel it would be accepting responsibility for damage done. They dismiss the whole problem by refusing to see the need for Alateen. For some people it is necessary to re-take the Fourth and Fifth Steps. For others, a comprehensive list, well pondered over, is recommended and will well repay the effort.

Becoming willing to make amends is the simplest part of this Step, I believe. Al-Anon people are not mean, vindictive creatures; they would never remain in the program were they such. So their first thought, when they realize what harm they have done, is regret for doing it and a wish to make amends. Thus they are ready to go forward to the next Step.

Discussion of the Ninth Step

"Made direct amends to such people wherever possible, except when to do so would injure them or others."

If we have earnestly, thoughtfully and prayerfully worked on the preceding eight, this Ninth Step goads us into action. We have recognized, and physically listed, those whom we have harmed. To stop there would be like breaking a leg but doing nothing about getting it set properly.

Direct amends frequently can be made: if we have harmed our families by neglect, ill-temper or harsh treatment, a change in attitude, conscientiously pursued, counterbalances the injuries. Or, if harm has come because we sloughed off work on others: refused Group, PTA or other responsibilities, on account of embarrassment or just sat back in selfish indolence, then we can make amends by accepting our full share of work in these common projects.

But many times direct amends seemingly are beyond us. For instance, the person hurt may be dead and it's too late. Or a loose tongue might have led us into intruding on someone's privacy by idle talk about a "slip" and we don't even remember the name. Also we may have completely lost touch with a person harmed, so that direct amends appear impossible.

Luckily amends still can be made in most instances because our Al-Anon responsibility is very like that of a parent: we never really requite our parents for all they have done for us but we do pay our debt to them by being the best parent possible to our children.

Our new book says, "Al-Anon responsibility is forward." That forward responsibility covers any situation where direct amends can not be made: if we have harmed one person in the past, we can help one, ten or a thousand in the present and in the future, by actively living and practicing the Al-Anon program.

Discussion of the Tenth Step

"Continued to take personal inventory and when we were wrong promptly admitted it."

Normal daily living involves constant repetition of various activities: eating, sleeping, bathing, work of all sorts and diversions to renew our spirits. Therefore it should surprise no one that living our program is not, and never will be a one-time effort.

To be successful in this program we have to take and re-take most of the Twelve Steps. Human frailty erodes the best resolve to live by them unless we constantly keep aware of a tendency to relax our vigilance and to prattle, "I know the Steps—they are a wonderful way of life."

Yes, we did take a moral inventory in the Fourth Step, just as we ate breakfast this morning. But the breakfast we ate today won't carry us through tomorrow and the next day and the next. Neither will that one moral inventory.

The Tenth Step is just like breakfast. It extends the good we got from our original inventory. Because we are exposed to widely varying situations, we are also exposed to new temptations by them. We may not have to struggle with the same old faults and failures, but since we are not perfect we probably will have to struggle to shed new shortcomings.

But by the time we have come to the Tenth Step we are better armed to deal with these new defects of character. For one thing, most likely they are not as deep-seated and entrenched as previous failings, but probably they're there.

Effort put into overcoming long-established faults is a great help in uprooting new weeds in our Al-Anon gardens. But we can only rid ourselves of them if we are aware that they have sprung up.

To obtain that awareness, before the crop is well-established, we have to continue to take inventory. When wrong we must promptly admit it, but also we must encourage ourselves to keep trying, by crediting ourselves with progress made in overcoming faults . . . old and new.

This Tenth Step does not explicitly state this idea but to me it is clearly implied. There must be two sides to any balance sheet and we should assess our good points as well as our bad ones for what they are.

Discussion of the Eleventh Step

> *"Sought through prayer and meditation to improve our conscious contact with God as we understood Him, praying only for knowledge of His will for us and the power to carry that out."*

Some of you perhaps remember the old, childish saying, when a playmate refused to do as you wished, "I'm going to pick up my dolls and go home."

I'm sure I did pick up my things on occasion and went home. But I was a child then. I have been fortunate, as an adult, not to react that way when endless "gimme" prayers seemingly brought no answer to me.

Many others were not as lucky. They write that after long years of prayer, if the situation remained unchanged, they stopped believing in God. They decided He had no interest in them; they dropped Him from their lives and it took Al-Anon to bring them back to faith.

Such an attitude by adults, seems to me today a lot like picking up your toys and going home in a pet. After all, what is the purpose of life if it is not growth? Are we to have everything our own way, exactly as we'd like it? Should we not allow others to grow and mature in theirs?

There are really only three answers to prayer: "Yes," "No," and "Wait a bit."

If our idea of God is that He is merely a source of goodies, and our responsibility to Him is to let Him give them, then it's easy to stop believing in Him when prayers repeatedly are answered with a No.

But no one can really spend much time on this Step and still cling to such a childish idea. In our own lives, with our children, we, for their best good, frequently have to deny their requests. Or we sometimes have to teach them to accept waiting for something until they are old enough to have it.

This Step helps us to the understanding that, by ourselves, we have made many mistakes. It takes a lot of faith, courage, and work on the earlier Steps to bring us to the realization that our own will has not been our best guide.

Once we accept, again or for the first time, that God is all-loving and cares for us as we do for our children, life gets easier. The closer we come to Him, the more knowledge of His will for us comes to us. With this knowledge comes the courage and power to carry it out.

Some one recently quoted a thought from an old FORUM which had been helpful. I hunted it up and found Pauline G., then WSD from Indiana, had read it somewhere and sent it in more than four years ago! It is most appropriate here!

"Many of us lose confidence in prayer because we do not realize the answer. We ask for strength and God gives us difficulties which make us strong. We pray for wisdom and God sends us problems, the solution of which develops wisdom.

"We plead for prosperity and God gives us brain and brawn with which to work. We plead for courage and God gives us dangers to overcome. We ask for favors and God gives us opportunities."

After all, if you feel you have lost contact with God, remember, Pascall says, "When you start looking for God, you have already found Him."

Discussion of the Twelfth Step

"Having had a spiritual awakening as the result of these Steps, we tried to carry this message to others, and to practice these principles in all our affairs."

You who like to take the Steps in their numerical order will find reassurance in the opening of this one. And those who prefer to jump around and perhaps skip one or two, might consider the wisdom of an orderly progression.

This Step says clearly that the spiritual awakening comes as the result of these Steps, which means the previous eleven—not two or three of them nor even six or seven; it may be worthwhile to give them more thought: to go back and make sure you have taken all of them.

Undoubtedly, if you work conscientiously on any of the Steps, you will be rewarded with a deepened spiritual awareness. But the spiritual awakening will be more complete, more lasting, if there are no blank spots in your approach to it.

Furthermore, if you have worked on all the Steps, it will be much easier for you to fulfill the second part of the Twelfth . . . that of practicing these principles in all your affairs.

Basically Al-Anon's whole program is built on the Twelfth Steps. If they are as integral a part of your consciousness as your own name and address, you will find it easier to live by them.

But if you continue, in spite of experience, to try to run your own life and that of your mate too, you'll continue to struggle in the dark, wondering why you are having so much trouble.

If you have taken the Fourth Step and let it go at that, you won't have benefited greatly. The next five need as much attention as the Fourth. And just to make sure there are no slips, there's always the Tenth Step to round out your working of the program.

There is so much satisfaction, such a sense of accomplishment, in giving a hand to someone going down for the third time, that some members rush into Twelfth Step work—that is, sharing the program with those in need of a mental or spiritual lift—as if that were the aim and entire end of this Twelfth Step.

Surely that is one part but, important as it is, it really is the topping, the strawberry jam on the peanut butter. The basic strength of Al-Anon's program comes from the spiritual awakening which results from honest work on all the preceding eleven and keeping at it.

Discussion of the First Tradition

"Our common welfare should come first; personal progress for the greatest number depends upon unity."

You doubtless remember the foreword to Al-Anon's Traditions: "Group experience indicates that the unity of the Al-Anon Family Groups depends upon adherence to these Traditions."

Thus, at the start, the purpose of our Traditions is spelled out. We have the responsibility to make certain that Al-Anon's program will endure throughout the world.

The program necessarily relies upon members working for our common welfare. "If a house be divided against itself, that house cannot stand." Lincoln staked his career on this statement: "I believe this government cannot endure permanently, half slave and half free." These truths do not change.

Certainly unity is of vital importance but it still is typical of Al-Anon's broad program that there are no *musts* in the Traditions. On the contrary, they are full of *mays, shoulds, oughts* and *we needs*.

Just as the Twelve Steps provide guidance for individual members, the Twelve Traditions provide guidance to safeguard groups.

This first Tradition shows clearly that the Al-Anon fellowship is and should be, more important than any individual member. If we were split apart by a dozen different practices and interpretations of the program, there soon would be no chance for personal progress.

Therefore it should not be difficult for each of us to keep constantly aware that we are only a tiny (although important) part of a huge fellowship. We should not force personal views upon other members nor try to run our group to suit ourselves.

Each member needs his own place in the sun so that he may grow spiritually in the program. He'll never get that place if he is continually overshadowed.

Groups which regularly review the Traditions, devote time to discuss them earnestly, seldom encounter the problem of a Mr. or Mrs. Al-Anon dominating the group.

Successful groups stem from a faithful observance of this First Tradition because it engenders a spirit of unity and fair play which gives each member his opportunity to grow—at his own pace.

Discussion of the Second Tradition

"For our group purpose there is but one authority—a loving God as He may express Himself in our group conscience. Our leaders are but trusted servants; they do not govern."

Al-Anon's program is a spiritual one, not confined to any race, creed or religious discipline. Why then is God brought directly into five of the Twelve Steps, indirectly (Power greater than ourselves which is God to some of us) into another and again into this Second Tradition?

I think the answer is because everyone believes in something. Atheists believe in their unbelief; agnostics, while not believing in an actual God, are willing to concede He might exist if it could be proved. And the rest of us have our own faiths, all quite apart from Al-Anon.

Al-Anon's Steps leave everyone free to acknowledge God "as we understood Him" and this Tradition specifies a "loving God as He may express Himself in our group conscience." Thus there is no religious difficulty about that. For unbelievers, the group conscience is the motivating force.

And think what a safeguard the group conscience is for the Al-Anon Family Groups. One member may misinterpret some part of the philosophy; one or two may go off at a tangent which some day, left unchecked, might be disrupting. This easily could happen if groups affiliated with other causes or movements.

But with the group conscience as a guide, it's difficult to see how a whole group could go wrong. The group conscience is simply an extension of that old, reliable "two heads are better than one." Thus far it has kept our fellowship hewing to the line and provided wise counsel for us all.

Lastly, this Tradition enjoins us to maintain the strict equality which exists, or should exist, in Al-Anon. We have no ruling caste; those responsible for carrying on program and group activities are there to serve the group, not to run it for personal aggrandizement.

Al-Anon's program is one for the ages. The Steps and Traditions keep it so.

Discussion of the Third Tradition

> *"The relatives of alcoholics, when gathered together for mutual aid, may call themselves an Al-Anon Family Group, provided that, as a group, they have no other affiliation. The only requirement for membership is that there be a problem of alcoholism in a relative or friend."*

This Third Tradition is double-barreled—both inclusive and exclusive; furthermore, it implies considerably more than it explicitly states.

To qualify for an Al-Anon Family Group, it is not enough for relatives of alcoholics to gather together. They so gather together for mutual aid and in addition they do not dissipate their efforts by diluting their primary purpose with other causes.

Groups do not meet to allow harried relatives of alcoholics to let off steam by discussion of alcoholic behavior. They meet to give aid and mutual understanding to each other, to enable members to live more peaceably and quietly with an active problem, or to help members repair the damage they have done to themselves through ignorance of the disease.

This damage frequently persists, and sometimes grows worse for a time, after the alcoholic has become sober. Too many spouses have pinned all their hopes and all their faith on the idea that the only thing needed was for the spouse to stop drinking and the millennium would begin. Sometimes it does begin with sobriety; sometimes the situation is worsened: some non-alcoholic spouses expect too much too soon; some fail to make allowance for the fact that neither party is starting fresh and rested—the alcoholic is pursued with haunting remorse and a shaky hold on a precarious and far-from-complete grasp of the AA program, while the mate is hagridden by persistent memories of endless broken promises, disappointments and distrust of continued sobriety.

If the group had another affiliation or purpose as well as Al-Anon, its efforts could be diverted and divided and fewer would be able to find any degree of serenity.

As to membership, the requirement is very explicit, ". . . problem of alcoholism in a relative or friend." Here again, more is implied: some very conscientious members occasionally question their eligibility for membership in a group if their alcoholic spouse or relatives dies.

It seems to me there is no question here whatever. They came to Al-Anon for help with an alcoholic problem; damage done by alcoholism drove them to it. They found the help they needed in the Al-Anon Group. If that need persists, even after the death of the alcoholic, it seems only logical they still are eligible to be members.

Moreover they frequently can contribute much that is valuable to the group, so that they actually give more than they receive. But even if they didn't, it seems to me they still are welcome members. Our purpose is to give help, hope and understanding to those who have suffered from problems of living with, or having lived with, alcoholism.

I believe Al-Anon's hospitable doors should always be open to anyone who comes to it for help where alcoholism is the root of one's difficulty. Death does not always end all problems nor, to me, does it end Al-Anon's responsibility for stretching out the helpful hand of fellowship.

Discussion of the Fourth Tradition

"Each group should be autonomous, except in matters affecting another group or Al-Anon or AA as a whole."

This Tradition is the simplest of the Twelve. Explicitly stated as it is, it seems difficult to believe there ever could be any misunderstanding of it. However, misunderstanding actually has arisen occasionally in the past.

One example of what almost happened, when insufficient consideration was given to plans for a public presentation of Alateen, clearly shows the vital necessity to our program of this Tradition. It further points up the scrupulous care needed to carry out the Tradition.

An overzealous sponsor, rightly proud of a remarkably fine group of youngsters, planned to present a typical meeting on television as a means of informing, impressing and interesting other teenagers living with alcoholic problems. He planned to have the participants sit in a half-circle, facing the screen!

It was only by the Grace of God that someone outside the group learned of the plan in time to call the sponsor's attention to this Fourth Tradition and to the Eleventh and Twelfth as well.

Just for a moment think of how many anonymities would have been broken had half a dozen youngsters faced that television screen! Perhaps some of the parents, AA and Al-Anon, and other relatives, would not have cared much, if at all. But many more in all likelihood would have been deeply upset.

Granted that the sponsor had planned the program, not for personal glory but to spread the word of Alateen, he definitely had given no consideration to how such a presentation would affect other Alateen groups, Al-Anon and AA.

Alcoholism for long was considered a stigma. AA, Al-Anon and Alateen work hard to get it accepted as "a disease and not a disgrace." It is little wonder that new-comers in all three fellowships are frequently greatly concerned to make their membership as little obtrusive as possible. They usually become less tense about it as time goes on but still, anonymity is the basis of the program and they have been assured theirs will be protected.

Had the sponsor given due consideration to these three all-important Traditions, he would have planned from the beginning to present the meeting as it actually was done, with the unidentified youngsters behind a screen.

We have about the widest latitude possible in our fellowships. No one wants to hedge us about with rules. But it is imperative that we safeguard everyone by giving careful thought to where our own freedom ends and that of others begins. Especially is this needful when a group considers branching out.

A large part of Al-Anon's rapid growth has stemmed from our meticulous observance of this Fourth Tradition.

Discussion of the Fifth Tradition

"Each Al-Anon Family Group has but one purpose: to help families of alcoholics. We do this by practicing the Twelve Steps of AA ourselves, by encouraging and understanding our alcoholic relatives, and by welcoming and giving comfort to families of alcoholics."

This Tradition, like the other eleven, goes straight to the point. There is no pussyfooting, no equivocation, no detouring into side issues. It tells us decisively that Al-Anon Family Groups have only one purpose: it defines that purpose and gives definite explanations of how we can accomplish it.

First, by practicing the Twelve Steps. This is not easy to do. It was a lot simpler for us to admire them as a way of life for the alcoholic—as many of us did at first. But when we accepted them as our own way of life, when we shouldered our own responsibility for governing our lives by practicing them faithfully, we soon learned that we were abundantly rewarded for our efforts.

Second, by encouraging and understanding the alcoholic. This is even more difficult than the Steps. In fact, if I am to be honest, I find it impossible to understand more than that there is an absolute compulsion to drink after even the smallest amount of alcohol has been drunk. I don't have that compulsion; I so hate feeling the least bit ill that even contemplating the hangovers, black-outs and all the other complications of drinking too much, would scare me into letting liquor alone.

Fortunately, I believe, just understanding this much is enough. Full understanding comes from one alcoholic to another.

The best encouragement we can give alcoholics comes

from the improvement we make in ourselves and the calmer, hands-off climate we establish in our homes, through Al-Anon.

Third, by welcoming and giving comfort to families. Those of us who have found Al-Anon, with its blessed restoration of hope, courage and serenity, know that the most important thing in our lives is to keep close to Al-Anon always, so that we may share the blessings of it with others in need. All that we have learned in our fellowship, I believe, would be Dead Sea fruit if we kept it for ourselves and did not pass it on to others in need, in gratitude.

Discussion of the Sixth Tradition

"Our Al-Anon Family Groups ought never endorse, finance or lend our name to any outside enterprise, lest problems of money, property and prestige divert us from our primary spiritual aim. Although a separate entity, we should always cooperate with Alcoholics Anonymous."

One of Al-Anon's greatest safeguards is explicitly stated in the opening phrases of this Tradition, with the specific reason for the admonition immediately following.

The wisdom of such a policy is very evident when you consider that the Al-Anon Family Group movement is worldwide—international in a very real sense. Al-Anon's priceless unity stems from this Tradition.

That unity would be seriously jeopardized if groups in South Dakota and South Africa spent half their time sponsoring local issues. If groups in Alberta, Australia and Argentina endorsed measures peculiar to their localities, there'd be every opportunity for politics to divide their membership. Were Al-Anon linked to any party, there'd be every chance it would lose prestige should that party fall into disrepute.

Al-Anon's primary aim, its very reason for being, is here defined as a spiritual one. You'd run into constant difficulties in keeping it spiritual if you diluted that program by mixing in worldly or material considerations particularly characteristic of your own communities. Our problem, that of learning to live with problems connected with alcoholism, is a universal one. We all do well to address our entire effort to this one subject.

The second sentence of this Tradition very properly follows the first one. We are not now, never have been and very likely never will be an integral part of Alcoholics Anonymous. The AA fellowship has enough on its own hands for it to insist that it remain separate from anything else . . . just as Al-Anon does.

Although Al-Anon is not affiliated with AA in any way, AA has cooperated with us magnificently. Without their members' help, their example and their generosity in sharing their experience, Al-Anon never could have attained such remarkable growth in so short a time.

There should be no resentment, no hurt feelings, that AA did not welcome Al-Anon into its fellowship. I do not believe any such feelings of misunderstanding now exist. AA's program is for alcoholics—Al-Anon's for living with alcoholism. We in Al-Anon are fortunate that theirs came first and they shared it so generously with us.

The debt, of each and every one of us, is great and only can be repaid by cooperating in every way we can.

Discussion of the Seventh Tradition

"Every group ought to be fully self-supporting, declining outside contributions."

Besides being the shortest of the Twelve Traditions, this one should be one of the simplest and easiest to understand. However there are frequent questions about it.

The most recent was answered in the Ask-It-Basket session of the Conference: Should tickets to an Al-Anon dance, dinner or party be sold to outsiders when a group wishes to raise money?

The answer was no, since it would jeopardize the anonymity of AA spouses, some of whom wouldn't care but others would object. Under our Tradition of cooperating with AA and guarding members' anonymity, such affairs should be kept within the fellowship.

Groups really need little money: enough to buy literature, pay rent, buy coffee and cake for meetings, support intergroups (if any), Assemblies and World Service work—those are the usual commitments. One very helpful expense that groups could undertake is to maintain a Post Office Box so that a permanent mailing address can be assured. Such a box would save both time and money at WSO in changing group records every time there is a new Secretary.

The reasoning behind this Tradition is clear, patterned as it is after AA's. It is the age-old idea that "he who pays the piper calls the tune." We could endanger our primary purpose of following Al-Anon's program, were we to accept support by government, civic organizations or philanthropists. We'd perhaps risk pressure being brought to include things other than learning to live with the problem of alcoholism.

There are times when it is tempting to accept outside bequests. So much good could be done with a gift of a thousand or more dollars, freely given. Al-Anon has always refused, although with gratitude, such legacies and gifts. Under this Tradition, Al-Anon always will refuse them and will be the stronger for it.

Discussion of the Eighth Tradition

"Al-Anon Twelfth-Step work should remain forever nonprofessional, but our service centers may employ special workers."

One of Al-Anon's greatest safeguards is assured by this Tradition. It provides against commercialization of the program.

"Carrying the message to others" by volunteers has a thousand better chances of acceptance by a troubled person than if it were offered by professionals who make their living at it. It would be difficult to question the motive of a person who freely shares his own experience with the sole purpose of helping another.

Furthermore there is no need in Al-Anon for professional Twelfth Step workers. Part of our philosophy and our obligation in Al-Anon is to share the same enlightenment, understanding and hope we ourselves have gained from the program.

If we try to bottle it all up within ourselves, to hoard it and to forget that there are others still in darkness and despair, we reap only a fraction of Al-Anon's benefits. The program stagnates within us; we stunt our own growth. We have to share what we have gained in order to keep it.

It is in freely sharing that we strengthen our belief and our reliance on the program. We cannot idly chatter when we are intent upon making another person understand our philosophy. Rather, we have to put our minds upon just what those factors are which make the program work for us.

It is a constant re-evaluation process we use when we review our own experiences to enable us to select exactly those things we used successfully in cases like those of the persons we try to help.

It wouldn't help any spouse to be told he or she had worsened a bad situation by trying to control and manage the alcoholic's life, unless you can show what *you* did which was useless and stupid. You cannot get anyone to stop harming those about him unless *you* can show exactly what harm has been done and how.

In essence, every good Twelfth Step job involves a review, conscious or subconscious, of your own life in Al-Anon.

Since spreading the word of Al-Anon is so vital a part of the program, the second part of this Tradition is necessary. The movement began when Lois W. and Annie S. first worked with widely scattered groups of AA wives who met to practice the AA program for themselves.

There were a few established groups before 1951. Bill W. had learned of them when he made a trip across the United States and Canada to instil an interest in an AA Conference.

He returned home most enthusiastic about these groups but feared they might go their own separate ways if there weren't some central unifying office. Two volunteers, Lois and Anne B., worked seven months alone until the correspondence became too heavy. They moved their work-base to Manhattan so that others would help to lighten their load. Volunteers came—and more volunteers—and Al-Anon grew.

Very shortly, in three years or less, Al-Anon growth had so increased that volunteers could no longer handle it and the beginnings of today's fulltime staff were established. With all the world to deal with, mostly by correspondence of one kind or another, these special staff workers are now essential to maintain and foster further growth. The World Service Center could not run without them.

Intergroups find themselves in the same situation. A few loyal volunteers can supply the need in the beginning. But growth is attained at such a rapid pace in most cases that special workers must be employed.

Al-Anon, taking the lead from AA, has been wise enough to distinguish between and provide for the two kinds of Al-Anon work: Twelfth Step work, always non-professional and unpaid—clerical work, professional and paid when needed.

Discussion of the Ninth Tradition

"Our groups, as such, ought never be organized; but we may create service boards or committees directly responsible to those they serve."

This Tradition is probably responsible for an ever-recurring nightmare to many jittery Al-Anon members who are apprehensive that any change, big or little, may endanger a program which has brought so much good to them. That one word, "organized," I believe, is the culprit, if a word doing the job for which it was chosen could be called a culprit.

Al-Anon, like AA, is a fellowship in which every member in every group is free to take what he likes and ignore what he doesn't. Al-Anon operates according to the

Golden Rule and our limitations are only those which keep us from hurting others or infringing upon their rights.

If it was a political organization we'd have a head, charged with keeping us in line with party policy; trying to influence our support for party office-holders and aspiring candidates for office. We'd be either majority "ins" or minority "outs," depending upon who had won the last election and was temporarily in power.

But in Al-Anon there is no power, no musts except those we make for ourselves. We do have certain leaders but their duties are limited and so is their term of office.

Our groups need Chairmen to plan and keep order at meetings; usually they are chosen for six months or at most a year. Treasurers are elected for a like period for the usual duties; some groups have Secretaries while others combine this office with that of Treasurer.

Group Representatives are essential to keep contact with Area Committees, Assemblies and to act as FORUM representatives. Where groups have special interests, such as Institutional and Public Relations work, Committee Chairmen are elected or appointed.

Our World Service Office functions as a liaison center for groups all over the world, to foster their growth and unity. It has no power to say, "This must be done." Because of its unique position as the working center for 4,500-plus groups with their wealth of experience, it is able to draw attention to and caution against certain practices which have been found to lead to trouble in the past. But it is in no way a gigantic policeman, nightstick in hand, to threaten a group's autonomy.

Nothing much but size has changed in the Al-Anon Family Groups in nearly two decades. Probably nothing ever will since we have chosen as our one authority a "loving God as He may express Himself in our group conscience."

Al-Anon constantly strives to broaden the base of those who carry on its work: the old Advisory Board was replaced nine years ago by the annual Conference of Delegates from all over the United States and Canada. We have been fortunate these past two years in having a Representative from the United Kingdom present to give us the benefit of their Al-Anon experience.

We now have a Regional Trustee from the Western United States on our Board of Trustees and look forward to another from Eastern Canada next year and a third from the Eastern U.S. the year after. They, it is hoped, will bring special experience and skills to enhance our work.

All this "creating of service boards and committees" is not organization in the political sense. Ask yourself how otherwise so much could have been done as well in so short a time?

Al-Anon has been fortunate in finding the people it needs to carry on its work as it should be carried on. With the safeguards provided in our Twelve Traditions, it seems reasonable to expect it will always be as fortunate.

Discussion of the Tenth Tradition

> "The Al-Anon Family Groups have no opinion on outside issues; hence our name ought never be drawn into public controversy."

Double-barreled shotguns are fine for giving one a quick second shot at moving objects going in different directions. But Al-Anon's ends are better served by concentrating all its ammunition toward the fixed targets of its threefold purpose.

"To welcome and give comfort to the families of alcoholics; to give understanding and encouragement to the alcoholic in the home; and to grow spiritually through living by the Twelve Steps of AA."

Even a cursory consideration of those three purposes shows they are important enough and compelling enough to stand alone—not to be mixed with diverse interests which would dilute our efforts.

Faithful practice of the Al-Anon program extends the range of every practicing member. Where he has lived with fear, distrust and despair, Al-Anon's program sets him free, not only to live his own life confidently but to give understanding assistance and strength not only to the tottering newcomer, wavering between hope and despair, but to all who need it.

There is no place in Al-Anon for official recognition of political or religious connections. Al-Anon Family Groups designedly limit their scope to handling problems caused solely by alcoholism.

As individual human beings we can, if we desire, believe that the world is flat, that eating meat is harmful, that the government should bring up all children and be responsible for everyone from the cradle to the grave. But if we involve ourselves in outside issues, we do so only as private individuals, not as Al-Anon members.

If I personally believe that astronomical expenditures for space exploration is wanton extravagance amounting practically to a swindle of public funds which could be better used to find a cure for the common cold, that is my right. But I am not free to organize an "Al-Anon Stop The Space Program Movement." I could, if anyone can imagine it, become a Carrie Nation and join a Temperance Union.

But I am not free to hitch it to our fellowship and make it an "Al-Anon Family Group Temperance Union."

Just as long as Al-Anon Family Groups remain faithful to carrying out the three avowed purposes for which they were designed, as long as they do not dissipate Al-Anon strength on divisive issues, they will continue to grow and flourish. They will continue to be the bulwark they now are for so many needful thousands around the world.

Discussion of the Eleventh Tradition

"Our public relations policy is based on attraction rather than promotion; we need always maintain personal anonymity at the level of press, radio, TV and films. We need guard with special care the anonymity of all AA members."

This three-part Tradition demands consideration lest it become a stumbling block for the unwary. Each word is a simple one. Each point is perfectly clear. But all too often one point or another is tossed into a discussion of some proposed action as a reason for maintaining the status quo.

Take the "attraction rather than promotion" phrase. A lot of comfortable, let-George-do-it inertia can hide behind those words when an energetic, inspired Al-Anon member suggests that meeting time and place be advertised; when visits to doctors, judges, clergymen and others are proposed; or when a series of instructive newspaper articles is suggested.

Al-Anon's first purpose is to welcome and give comfort to the families of alcoholics. Nothing in this Tradition says this welcome and comfort is to be extended only by word of mouth to persons known to us. Nothing prohibits a newspaper announcement, an educational campaign to instruct the public on what Al-Anon Family Groups are.

It has always seemed to me that this situation is vividly illustrated by an old-time sailing master who needed to fill out his crew. He had two ways to do it: to list the jobs with information of pay, privileges and the benefits of life at sea. That, to me, was attraction—what we do when we try to reach those in need whom we do not know personally.

But when the captain hired press gangs to set upon drunken seamen or knock solitary wayfarers unconscious and shanghai them for forced service aboard his ship, he resorted to promotion.

Attraction, to me, is giving a choice of whether or not one eats by making food look, taste and smell appealingly or has it crammed down the throat with pumpguns as they do with Strasbourg geese when they raise them for paté de foie gras.

"At the level of press, radio, TV and films" is the motivating phrase of this Tradition. Some members are so impressed with the necessity for anonymity they overlook just why and where anonymity is good. Our Conference Approved pamphlet, "Why Is Al-Anon Anonymous?" makes a clear distinction between anonymity inside and outside the Al-Anon Family Groups.

We do not furtively slink in and out of meetings, put paper bags over our heads or issue masks to group members. Under this Tradition we speak freely, confident that nothing said in an Al-Anon meeting will be repeated outside.

Both Al-Anon and AA have benefited greatly from the press, radio, TV and films. Without their support, their generous help in bringing word of our fellowships to great masses of people, neither could have attained the growth

they enjoy today. Without them, thousands upon thousands
would still be suffering, searching for help.

Both Al-Anons and AAs speak freely, intimately and
confidently at large meetings where these media are well
represented. Their trust has never been abused when the
Tradition of anonymity has been made clear to the press.
It is only when a chairman has not explained the value and
seriousness of guarding anonymity that some unfortunate
incidents have occurred.

Our debt to Alcoholics Anonymous is so great, we'd
make a poor return for all it has given us if we carelessly
disregarded the third part of this Tradition which enjoins
us to "guard with special care" the anonymity of all AA.

Just as we leave the drinking problem to the alcoholic,
so do we leave the degree of AA anonymity to the alcoholic.

Discussion of the Twelfth Tradition

*"Anonymity is the spiritual foundation of all our Tradi-
tions, ever reminding us to place principles above personalities."*

Human nature never has been noted for perfection.
Most of us have a great need to grow spiritually, to overcome mistakes made in the past and to learn how such
mistakes can be avoided in the future.

For persons who have been adversely affected by problems of living with alcoholism, the Al-Anon Family Group
program is as much of a "specific" as quinine for treating
malaria. But Al-Anon's treatment is not one of pills or
tablespoonfuls "to be taken every four hours." Rather it is
one of helping ourselves and others by living the Al-Anon
Steps and Traditions.

Entirely putting aside our obligation to protect the anonymity of our alcoholic mates, there would be little chance for spiritual growth were we to call attention to ourselves with constant reminders, broadcast at large, that we are following the Al-Anon program and that it is one of self-improvement.

If friends question a change in us because of our improved attitude, because we have finally matured a bit, have stopped being hypercritical, despondent and unduly anxious, then is the time to give credit to Al-Anon, person-to-person, not a public announcement for personal glory.

One of our greatest obligations, as well as joys, is to give hope and help to others in like circumstances who are struggling along alone. Surely our opportunities for such giving would be cut to a minimum if we seemed to present ourselves publicly as saviors of mankind, models of rectitude.

With anonymity as the spiritual base of our program, there is little danger we'll relapse into our old ways of thinking ourselves the center of the universe. We'll constantly be reminded of the hard-earned humility we have gained. We'll be glad to content ourselves with growth and let our light shine from within, rather than to bask in the limelight.

With this humility laboriously gained from self-discipline, it will be much easier for us to practice the second part of this Tradition: to place principles above personalities.

There was a time when our minds were so full of our own affairs, our disappointments, our opinions and desires, that we seldom listened to anyone; we especially ignored those who differed with us.

But Al-Anon's program, which taught us so clearly how powerless we are over many things, taught us to recognize the things we could change and those we couldn't. And it also taught us to listen. In listening, we sometimes learned that even those persons we didn't much care for, frequently had ideas worth listening to. We no longer could afford judgments on the basis of whether or not we liked or admired a person.

"Principles above personalities" is another exercise in humility and putting principles first also makes for spiritual growth.

Index of Subjects

You will find this listing of the subjects covered in our book a big help, both in planning meetings and for your personal needs.

Acceptance: 47, 83, 117, 120, 138, 154, 163, 173, 174, 183
Al-Anon: As a Fellowship: 3, 86, 121, 198
    As a Way of Life: 6, 9, 33, 37, 40, 47, 106, 140, 174, 193
    How started: 91
    Literature (Conference-Approved): 147
    Purposes: 2, 19, 48, 73, 124, 161, 196
Alcoholism, A Disease: 24, 62, 63, 68, 125, 145, 196
Amends: 108
Anger: 65, 207
Changing Ourselves: 5, 29, 130
Children: 8
Detachment: 116
Discouragement: 66, 67, 122, 169, 171
Expectations: 57, 61
Faith: 31, 43, 44, 96, 190
Fear: 31, 60, 81, 82, 96, 149, 174, 175, 190, 191
Forum: 94, 95
Frustration: 82
Giving: 40, 65, 152, 153, 157
Gratitude: 112, 133
Helping the Alcoholic: 93
Hope: 31, 43, 131, 141, 152, 153
Kindness: 25, 88
Meetings: 9, 70, 89, 90, 113, 114, 115, 125, 140, 141
Open Mind: 223, 224
Patience: 76
Perfection: 28, 69, 109
Prayer: 28, 29, 34, 42, 63, 64, 127, 215
Problem Solving: 11, 80, 99, 187
Recovery in Al-Anon: 1, 31, 49, 60, 93, 191
Rejection: 22
Resentments: 35, 36, 65, 148
Self Discipline: 56
Self Esteem: 14
Self-Knowledge: 45, 46
Self-Pity: 15, 16, 165, 200, 201
Selfishness: 226
Serenity: 25, 46, 47, 109, 147, 185
Serenity Prayer: 81, 84, 151, 167, 168, 208, 210, 211
Sharing: 18, 89, 94, 101, 202
Slips: 17, 54, 68, 180
Speaking: 89, 90, 113, 114, 115
Spiritual Growth: 55, 72, 100
Strength: 51

Talks: 12, 38, 39, 75, 76, 89, 101, 113, 155, 202
Tension Relievers: 59, 118, 146
Tolerance: 27
Understanding: 105, 125, 126
Wisdom: 144

Slogans: In general: 190, 191
   But For the Grace of God: 213
   Easy Does It: 26, 65, 146, 191, 217
   First Things First: 62, 66, 104, 191, 221
   Just For Today: III
   Let Go and Let God: 34, 59, 143, 191, 218
   Listen and Learn: 216
   Live and Let Live: 27, 28, 191, 224
   One Day At a Time: 32, 87, 119, 128, 156, 191, 214
   Think: 53, 84, 103, 104, 219

Steps: In general: 16, 71, 72, 73, 181
   1: 105, 106, 115, 117, 228
   2: 132, 231
   3: 21, 215, 232
   4: 108, 234
   5: 236
   6: 237
   7: 238
   8: 240
   9: 241
  10: 128, 181, 242
  11: 20, 127, 215, 244
  12: 67, 68, 74, 137, 139, 152, 158, 205, 246

Traditions:
   1: 135, 247   7: 227, 257
   2: 249   8: 258
   3: 250   9: 260
   4: 252   10: 262
   5: 254   11: 264
   6: 255   12: 266